Recovering After Hidden Abuse

What The Victims Need to Know to Recognize the Signs of Psychological Abuse and Recovery from Mental Manipulation - Includes Emotional Abuse and Narcissistic Abuse

Hayden Hanson, Rebecca Solis

Table of Contents

Emotional Abuse

Recognize the Signs of Psychological Abuse and Recovery from Mental Manipulation

Hayden Hanson

10

Introduction

E motional abuse is very misunderstood and often thought of as a "mild" form of abuse. It usually goes unrecognized because there are no physical bruises to show for it. It can take any form but is typically recognized through a pattern of intimidation, humiliation, anger, or emotional terrorism—the manipulation of a person's thoughts and emotions by an abuser until they are unable to think clearly or act independently while also feeling ashamed and guilty for being abused.

Now the first question I frequently hear is, "why call it emotional abuse? Because when I think of abuse, I think of physical." However, emotional abuse can be just as damaging, if not more so than physical. Emotional abuse can destroy your self-esteem, mental health and cause you to have major trust issues.

Now let's consider what a pattern is. Many people display abusive behavior at one time or another - and they may even be verbal or emotionally abusive on a daily basis - yet this does not mean they are emotionally abusing the other person. Emotional abuse is usually displayed through a pattern of controlling behaviors designed to manipulate the abuser's partner into doing what he/she wants.

Emotional abusers may make you feel like you are the crazy one. No matter how valid your feelings are or how much he/she was at fault, the abuser will tell you that you overreacted. The abuser will minimize and invalidate your feelings until you doubt yourself and start to believe that you are a "crazy" or over-sensitive person who must be wrong about what is going on in the relationship.

The abuser may even try to convince others of it, including friends, family members, and professionals such as counselors, clergy, or doctors.

It's not uncommon to find out later that a narcissist's most commonly used tool in gaining total control over his victim is other people. If one supports the narcissist, he may find people who can tell or make him believe they support him. This is done especially if the victim has no support system and/or is isolated from friends or family. The abuser will have people in his circle who will bad-mouth and even threaten to expose the victim using any tactic they can think of.

The victim will likely be told that if he leaves the relationship that he is crazy, then at least have a "little respect for him." He may also be threatened with verbal abuse, warnings of harm, or even death threats. (This usually takes place after an attempt to leave. The abuser knows that most abusers will attempt to get their victim back.)

After leaving, the victim is almost always punished. Most abusers spend time looking for new victims while in another relationship. They may act like victims themselves (victim-playing) or even come on strong by appearing to be apologetic and contrite about how bad they were. This is often referred to as "hoovering" after the popular Hoover vacuum cleaners. Just as you can't vacuum up a pile of dust and dirt without first tearing it apart, the abuser will try to find someone who was not completely flattened so they can have another go at destroying an innocent person's sense of self-worth.

Only those who have experienced this type of abuse will know what it is like to be treated so poorly because that type of treatment is reserved only for the abuser's partner - and even then, the abuser may also do such things to his own family members or others he sees as beneath him.

This book will explain the dynamics of various forms of abuse in varying levels in extreme detail and give your insight into how abusers change.

The book will also help you see through his games, recognize his tactics and tell you how to effectively protect yourself from further abuse.

This book is for victims who want to regain control over their lives, reclaim their self-worth, heal and become stronger from the abuse that has been done to them.

It is specifically written for women who have suffered at the hands of emotionally abusive men. It strives to reveal the signs and tell you what is happening; it guides you through the recovery process while helping you understand the behavior.

Chapter 1:

What is Abuse?

A buse can take various forms and includes not only physical violence but also sexual abuse, emotional abuse, neglect, and financial exploitation.

What is Abuse?

Abuse does not comprise only physical violence but also sexual abuse, emotional abuse, neglect, and financial exploitation.

Common Types of Abuse:

1. Emotional Abuse

Emotional abuse is the most common type of domestic violence that is physical and mental abuse. In the early stages of a relationship, an emotional abuser might try to isolate their partner to prevent them from quitting the relationship or leaving on their own. The emotionally abusive partner might also frequently criticize their partner, and you will find they constantly compare you with others, for example, your ex-boyfriend or ex-girlfriend. If you are upset about something that has happened in your life, these comments will usually be followed by criticism as well.

2. Financial Abuse

Financial abuse is by far the most common type of abuse in relationships. It often takes place alongside other forms of abuse, and it may be that you do not even realize it is taking place. This type of abuse can take many different forms but is usually the misuse of credit cards, burglary, and breaking into bank accounts in order to steal money. This is a type of abuse that the victim does not always realize has taken place until it is too late, for example, when they are either charged with a crime or suddenly find themselves without money to pay for things as a result of the financial abuser's actions.

3. Physical Abuse

Physical abuse is the most commonly accepted type of abuse, and this is when the abuser threatens or uses violence against their partner. Physical abuse can also include destroying property, harming or killing pets, restricting a partner's access to medical care, or forcing them to use drugs or alcohol. This type of abuse can take place at any stage in a relationship and will often escalate over time if the victim does not recognize it for what it is and seek help.

4. Sexual Abuse

Sexual abuse is another very common form of domestic violence that takes place in relationships and can be rape, forcing sex after drugging someone, or sexual harassment such as forcing an unwilling partner to look at pornography.

Why Abuse Happens?

If you have been abused, it is very important to know why the abuse happened and how to prevent it from happening again. Abusers often have a history of abusive behavior that they do not realize until they become involved with an independent partner.

Abuse is a Learned Behavior

Abuse can be learned in many different ways; for example, people who are emotionally abusive were possibly abused themselves when young and learned how to treat others the same way they were treated as a child. To stop abusers from abusing in the future, it is important to understand what makes them behave this way.

When an abuser feels threatened or humiliated, they are more likely to act aggressively.

Abuse is usually a sign that someone feels powerless in their life, but you can empower yourself by leaving the relationship as fast as possible.

It is also important to be aware of the different stages in an abusive relationship, and this is particularly important when considering whether or not to take steps to stop abuse from happening or continuing.

Preventing Abuse:

• Recognizing Red Flags: If you know what some of the signs of abuse are, it will make it easier for you to leave before things get worse than they already are. If there is one thing people regret most, it's that they did not leave a relationship earlier when they had the chance.

• Taking Action: The sooner you leave an abusive relationship, the less likely it is that you will become seriously hurt. If at all possible, leave the relationship immediately if you recognize the signs of abuse for what they are.

• Establishing Boundaries: If you are in an abusive relationship, your partner will most likely be unwilling to accept that their behavior is wrong, and as a result, it will be important for you to establish boundaries with them. You can establish boundaries such as not allowing them to make decisions about money or property without consulting you first and outlining a plan should the abuser decide to become violent.

• Take the First Step: As a victim of abuse, it is important to take the first step of asking for help. It is sometimes too much to ask, but the most important thing you can do is to stay safe and away from your abuser.

Chapter 2:

What are the Signs of Abuse?

How do we know it's emotional abuse? When it is present under its covert nature, emotional abuse is sometimes hard to recognize because it happens in a relationship, in the link between two people. That's why we say that, in its most basic form, emotional abuse equals control. Defining and spotting control issues focuses on the goal of seeking out and stopping emotional abuse.

The signs of emotional abuse can be covert or overt, both to the abuser and the victim.

Overt Signs

Overt signs are the easiest to notice, in which case you may already have an idea of how to define the behavior you're seeing. Overt signs are anything that is outwardly and obviously abusive and damaging, such as yelling or swearing out loud in crowded spaces, like a restaurant, breaking personal property when escalating a dispute, throwing away your belongings, attacking or causing damage to pets, or disappearing for days without notice.

Covert Signs

The abused person often appears frightened of the abuser or fearful of angering or displeasing the abuser. . . . As a result, actions and access are very much controlled, and the person often seems to have no freedom or capacity to make any independent decisions.

Covert emotional abuse tends to take place behind closed doors.

The only outward signs of abuse may be in the behavior of the victim himself, such as displaying:

1. Loss of self-confidence

2. Depression or mental confusion

3. Trouble sleeping

4. Shame and withdrawal behaviors

5. Eating disorders

6. Physical depletion (low energy, extreme weight changes, or an unexplained, repetitive illness)

The use of sex as a tool to abuse others is very frequent; just to avoid an escalating argument that threatens to turn violent, many women will give in and have sex to calm the angry spouse down. Otherwise, they might be accused of being frigid or a lesbian or having affairs with other men. If this shortcut is preferred, it is at the high cost of feeling used as an object or depersonalized by this kind of body abuse.

Behavior that alternates between overt charm and covert cruelty can be very confusing, and it produces a state of disorientation in the spouse who never knows if the person coming through the door will be Dr. Jekyll or Mr. Hyde.

Why is it that, being abused so clearly visible, most people put up with abuse and continue with the relationship?

Some victims are scared of being alone. Often told that they can't survive without a spouse to take care of them, that they dare not try living independently. Moreover, there are still some societies that reject and devalue single women, considering them worthless if they are not able to "keep a man."

Financial and social considerations are giving way, at least in the United States, to a wider perspective on new and different ways of living. The percentage of people living single in individual housing arrangements is growing, which speaks volumes about the acceptance of single living as a respectable and valid option. Nobody is rejected for being single but rather is appreciated as an individual.

Leaving social perspectives aside, the notion that some part of human development must take place alone holds a lot of water. The hidden assumption lurking beneath emotional abuse is, "You are nothing without a partner, and any partner is better than none." This tool for control evaporates into thin air as long as the single person discovers the joy of being able to make decisions in accord with her own deepest desires.

Many victims also believe that society requires them to stay in a toxic relationship, at least "for the children's sake." The tragic result is that children who grow up in an abusive environment tend to accept such as the pattern for their future relationships, hence ensuring another generation follows this toxic cycle.

What are the indications of emotionally abusive behavior?

There are signs that can be discerned by watching the abuser's behavior. Let's say you want to test your partner (or a family member or a friend) for emotionally abusive behavior; ask yourself the following questions- does your partner exhibit ANY of the following behaviors?

- Frequently humiliates you based on your intelligence, personality, skills, or appearance

- Ridicules your opinions and ideas in public

- Put up a fuss about or physically stops you from seeing your family and friends

- Steamrolls over you during heated debates so that the blame is displaced onto you

- Controls the finances and hides his own expenses from you

- Shifts debt to you because of a made-up "obligation" to pay them

- Guilt-trips, threatens, insults, or otherwise obligates you into having sex

- Denies you sexual intimacy as punishment

- Threatens or harms your personal possessions (inanimate or animate, such as pets)

- Threatens or harms your children

- Insults you and then says, "It was just a joke."

- Humiliates you in public or in front of your or his friends

- Belittles you for holding certain beliefs or for your heritage

- Makes insulting comments about your race or social class

- Purposely denies you affection or approval when you ask for it

- Changes the subject or rolls his/her eyes during a "This is how I feel" conversation

- Gives you the silent treatment or simply walks away from you

- Threatens you with blackmail or secrets

- Seems to enjoy/get off on fighting and arguments

- Has a public "facade" and behavior that no one else but you see through

- Threatens you if you do something (intentional or not) to ruin his/her public image

- Tries to control your appearance (the way you dress or do your hair)

- Threatens to leave or throw you out

- Treats you like a servant or his property

- Lies or manipulates the truth to make you look bad

- Carries on affairs and/or harasses you about imagined affairs to shift the attention

- Tells you what to do instead of requesting

- Blames you or others for all his problems

- Acts oblivious to other people's feelings yet expects attention for the slightest instance of having his feelings hurt

- Says or promises good things (professing love, saying romantic things) but does things that hurt

Any of these behaviors, when exhibited repeatedly, constitute emotionally abusive behavior that causes psychological stress or trauma for the victim. They are about keeping the other person weak and under the control of the abuser.

A woman named Clara posted this in a forum for the emotionally abused, "I was going to nursing school, and each day was a discovery trip for my brain. I'd get back home and share my new ideas with my husband, only to have him dissect and destroy them with his "logical arguments. Only after several repetitions of this discouraging behavior did I learn to keep my ideas to myself. What was really a big surprise was to hear him, at a party four weeks later, explaining those same ideas to his friends, as if they were his own reflections!. Then and there, I understood how my own excitement about learning, going to school again, having my brain alive with theories, etc., was so threatening to him! What he was doing was trying to keep the learning of my brain under his control, so he was not left behind!"

However, perhaps this list of emotional abuse indicators is missing something. It is not exhaustive. Perhaps your suspicion about your partner is based on a particular action or behavior of his that is hard to define or pin down. Trust your own perceptions because if it feels painful, diminishing you, or somehow humiliating you, be sure that it is not a behavior intended to make you feel good, or support your growth.

Chapter 3:
The Effects of Emotional Abuses

When victims realize aggression, they experience shock. Up to this point, they do not suspect anything; perhaps they are even too trusting.

They feel confused and offended and feel everything "collapsed." The extent of the injury depends on the degree of surprise and the unpreparedness for the consequences of the perverse effect. During an emotional shock, the victim mixes feelings of suffering and anxiety; there is a feeling of violent interference, shock, powerlessness, and collapse, which some victims describe as psychic aggression: "It's like a fist punch!", "He said terrible words to me, and I feel like a boxer who is already on the floor, but they continue to beat him mercilessly."

Strange, but anger and indignation are rare, even after the victims decide to part with the aggressor. And anger could help liberation. Victims will complain about the injustice of their fate, but nevertheless, they will not rebel. Anger will appear later, and most often, it will be restrained, which means it will not be effective. To experience real, liberating anger, the victim needs to not be under the influence of the aggressor.

When victims begin to realize that they are being manipulated, they feel cheated, as if they were being targeted. They get the feeling that they were misled, that they are not respected. A little later, they finally became convinced that they were victims, that they had been manipulated, and lost their self-esteem because of that. They are ashamed of the actions provoked by the manipulation: "I had to start resisting earlier!", "Why didn't I see anything?"

Shame comes from realizing their pathological indulgence, which made possible violence on the part of the partner.

Sometimes people want to avenge themselves, but more often, they try to rehabilitate themselves, to restore their self-esteem. They expect an apology from their aggressor, which will not be.

Weakening of Protective Functions

When the stupor that the victim experiences during the period of perverse influence recedes, the person begins to feel obvious aggression. The protective abilities of a person are not unlimited; they gradually decrease. After a certain amount of stress, the ability to adapt disappears, and mental exhaustion sets in, more prolonged and more severe disorders occur.

Basically, it is at the stage of decompensation that victims come to us, psychiatrists. They have a general state of anxiety, psychosomatic disorders, or depression. In more impulsive people, decompensation can be expressed in the transition to violent actions, which can bring them to a psychiatric hospital. In the eyes of the aggressor, these disorders often seem to be an excuse for moral persecution.

It is surprising that, at this stage, when we offer employees who are persecuted in the workplace to stop work for a while, they very rarely agree: "If I stop work, it will be even worse! It will cost me dearly!" Fear makes you put up with everything and anything.

Such a depressive state is associated with mental exhaustion, with an excess of stress. Victims feel exhaustion, tiredness, and apathy. They are not interested in anything. They are unable to focus even on the simplest actions. They may have thoughts of suicide. The risk is especially great at the moment when the victims realize that they have been deceived and that nothing will help them regain the fullness of their minds. If, in such cases, suicide or attempted suicide occurs, this supports the perverted people's confidence that the partner was weak, that her mind was clouded, or that she was initially crazy, and that the aggression made her feel justified.

During aggression, a perverted person behaves in such a way as to appear omnipotent, demonstrating moral rigor and prudence. Because of this, the process of losing illusions about the partner exacerbates the state of the victim. In general, life events that can lead to a state of depression include not only the death of a loved one or a divorce but also the loss of an ideal or an overvalued idea. As a result, there is a feeling of uselessness, powerlessness, and defeat. The starting point leading to a state of depression is likely to be a feeling of defeat and powerlessness, humiliation and feeling cornered, then a difficult or dangerous situation.

During the moral persecution after the failure of numerous attempts to establish a dialogue with the aggressor, the victim experiences a state of permanent anxiety, which is supported by ceasing attacks. This condition precedes the onset of fear and constant expectation, the cure of which often requires additional medication.

In some victims, the reaction manifests itself physiologically (gastric ulcer, cardiovascular, skin diseases, etc.). The body responds to an encroachment on the psyche of the victim, which she did not suspect, but could lead to the destruction of her personality. Some people brought to this state lose weight and weaken. Psychosomatic disorders are not a direct result of aggression but a person's inability to resist it (no matter what a person does, it will be wrong, she will always be to blame).

The reaction of some victims comes down to a change in behavior that is a direct result of perverse provocations. This is expressed in vain attempts to force oneself to hear (for example, nervous attacks in public) or in violent actions against the aggressor, which will only serve as an excuse for the latter: "I warned you, he/she is in a terrible state!"

It is known that impulsive aggressiveness can lead to a cruel crime to the same extent as a predatory one, but it seems that people with an impulsive type of aggression are more at risk of committing a crime. Perverted people, to prove how bad their victim is, are ready to provoke in her violence directed against themselves.

Another consequence that is often neglected is the dissociation of personality (the more well-known term is "split personality.")

In the reference book of the Department of Natural Sciences, dissociation (bifurcation) of a person is defined as a violation of functions that, in the normal state, are not separable from each other, such as consciousness, memory, self-identification, or perception of the environment. This is a phenomenon of protection from fear, grief, or powerlessness after any traumatic event, which is so alien to a normal perception that the psyche either transforms it or expels it from the human mind. With the dissociation of personality, there is a

27

separation of what can be endured and what cannot be endured, leading to amnesia. The experience gained is filtered, thus bringing relief or partial protection.

The phenomenon of dissociation enhances the perverse effect and presents an additional difficulty that must be taken into account during therapy.

A Break-Up

Victims can respond in two ways to an increasingly clear threat: they submit to and acknowledge the superiority of the aggressor, allowing him to calmly continue his destructive activities; rebel and fight to leave. Submitting to too strong or too old influence, some people are not able to fight or leave. Sometimes they can consult a psychiatrist or psychotherapist, but at the same time immediately refuse any fundamental research. They just want to "hold the blow," transfer their enslavement without any special consequences and "save face." These people usually prefer medication. However, after a series of depressions, an overdose of tranquilizers, and toxic substances that can occur in the human body, and the psychiatrist will be forced to offer psychotherapy again.

Parting, if at all possible, always takes place at the initiative of the victim. The process of liberation from the aggressor is accompanied by bitterness and guilt on the part of the former victim, as perverted narcissistic people pretend to be abandoned victims, and in this, they find a new reason for violence. When a relationship is broken, perverted people consider their interests infringed and become picky, taking advantage of the fact that victims, trying to quickly end this process, are still ready to make any concessions.

In a couple, blackmail and pressure are carried out through the children, if any, or through court procedures regarding joint properties. In a professional environment, a case is often brought against a victim who can always be blamed for something, for example, if a person accidentally took home an important document. In any case, the aggressor complains that his interests are infringed on, although, in reality, it is the victim who loses everything.

Evolution

If the victim nevertheless succeeds at the cost of his own efforts to finally break off relations with the aggressor, it is still impossible to deny the dramatic consequences of the earlier life, in which the victim was reduced to the state of things. From this moment on, any memory or new event will be seen through the tinted lenses of her past experience.

The physical distance from the aggressor at first brings the victim a sense of freedom: "Finally, I can breathe freely!" After a period of shock, interest in work or leisure activities, curiosity towards the world or people, and other feelings still blocked by addiction reappear with time away from the aggressor. However, it is not without difficulties.

Some victims of moral persecution come out of it, only retaining bad memories that they can control, mainly cases of short exposure or violence outside the family. Many experience unpleasant moments of reminiscence of traumatic situations but put up with them.

Attempts to forget more often lead to the appearance of belated mental or somatic disorders, as if you suffered it through another's body, while the psyche was active and inaccessible to the influence of the aggressor.

Experienced violence can leave light consequences that practically do not interfere with normal social life. The victims' psyche seems unscathed, but at the same time, less specific symptoms remain, such as an attempt to conceal the experienced aggression.

Chapter 4:

Psychological Abuse

P sychological abuse is a form of abuse where the victim is exposed to psychological trauma. One of the challenges with psychological violence is that, unlike physical violence, there might not be physical scars as evidence. Psychological abuse happens each time the victim is subjected to emotional distress. In many cases, psychological abuse is accompanied by verbal or physical abuse.

Many people are victims of psychological abuse at some point in time, but they are never aware of it. Without proper understanding of yourself and what your life is about, you might never know when you are under attack. It also becomes difficult to come up with effective strategies you can use to cope with the trauma from such abuse.

While anyone is susceptible to this kind of abuse, women and children are the most affected by psychological abuse. The attacks target perceptions, feelings, and thoughts. Psychological abuse might not be physical, but the effect on the victim's persona is just as bad.

In a relationship with a narcissistic partner, there are several symptoms, reactions, and conditions that the victim might experience, which are signs of abuse. The narcissist conditions the victim by creating experiences in relationships, which have a negative impact on the victim. Here are some of the signs you might be suffering psychological abuse in your relationship:

- Intense insecurities – your abuser identifies your personal insecurities and, over time, uses them to put you down. Your insecurities grow stronger, and you cannot trust anyone.

- Disbelief in yourself – many victims' lives change for the worse because they no longer believe in themselves. Your confidence is eroded to a point where you can no longer trust your judgment.

- Incapability – victims of abuse who were once assured and competent in everything they do suddenly become incapable and uncertain about everything.

- Anxiety – you live a life of uncertainty and fear. You are constantly afraid something bad will happen. You don't trust good things because you believe the happiness is short-lived, and the worst is just right around the corner. You also feel emotionally drained and incapable of enjoying true happiness.

- Indecision – victims who were once grounded become indecisive, confused, and unable to trust anyone, not even themselves.

- Esteem issues – psychological abuse erodes your confidence. You cannot see yourself as anything better than what your abuser says you are. You shy away from the public, afraid that everyone sees the weaknesses in you.

These are the effects of psychological abuse. They manifest in different ways, but one thing is certain about them – they erode the very core of your being, your personality. If you cannot recognize yourself, how can someone else?

Psychological violence is meted out to victims in different categories. We will address five of the spheres of life where healthy relationships are important and how narcissists take everything away from you.

Children and Families

- Trust issues

Life is one big frightening place for a child raised by narcissists. Strings are attached to everything, especially love. Children need unconditional love; however, children of narcissistic parents grow up learning that there is always something attached to it. Such children grow up suspicious of affection. It becomes difficult for them to trust anyone, especially those who are getting too close to them (Keene & Epps, 2016).

Interestingly enough, while such children struggle to embrace genuine affection, they are drawn to toxic relationships and affection. This happens because the feelings shared in such relationships are those that are too familiar, they can relate. Toxic relationships become a comfortable place for such children.

It is easier for a child brought up in a narcissistic environment to trust a bad person disguised as their savior than it is for them to trust someone who is genuine and offers emotional stability.

Toxic people are an embodiment of the same challenges the children endured when growing up. Because their minds have been conditioned to embrace such instances, they are not afraid to interact with toxic people. They learn not to trust or not to trust too much – this is easier because they have done it all their life.

- Inability to commit

Children raised in a narcissistic environment struggle with commitment issues. When you meet them, at first glance, they seem like they are looking to establish commitment with someone. However, deep down, they fear commitment. These kids grow up alienated by the people closest to them, so it is difficult to commit to someone or something. Commitment for such children is often based on what feels right at the moment, not because they really want to commit.

Long-term relationships are not easy to get into because the feeling of being tied down to something is odd. When they encounter someone who truly loves them, it is unsettling because they have to open up about their vulnerabilities to this person, and they are not sure whether this person will stay or walk away. When you grow up alienated by family, stability and forever relationships become a fallacy to you.

Commitment to someone for such a child means that they are giving up control of their lives. Someone else is in charge of their emotions. Naturally, such children will go into defense mode to protect themselves from being hurt. They know the feeling; they have lived through it and cannot risk it again. When facing the prospect of an intense relationship, it is easier to withdraw, even without a reason. They find it easier to give up on someone who loves them than be with them and experience unconditional love.

- Hyperactive attunement

Hyperactivity is one of the symptoms victims of abuse learn to help them cope with their abuser. It helps them know when things are about to get messy. They are keen on subtle changes in the way the abuser responds to them. This makes them realize changes in facial expression, tone, and so forth. They can also identify contradictions between gestures and spoken words.

It is so exhausting to learn all this as a child. However, it is also important for them because it is the only survival technique they are aware of, which can help them avoid unnecessary pain. They grow up on the lookout for verbal, physical, and emotional cues from narcissistic parents and caregivers.

This defense mechanism helps them get through a lot and protects them from the unknown. However, it also breeds a sense of prediction, which can be very unsettling for someone who is genuine but does not know how to align their words and gestures. For the child, it might be impossible to control how people react, but they can use this technique to choose the relationships they can cultivate or end.

- Afraid of intimacy

Intimacy is an emotional minefield for children raised by narcissists. When they try to open up, it is easier to share too much about their struggles hoping that someone might genuinely feel and ease their pain. The challenge here is that they often end up with toxic narcissists whose only desire is to prey on their weaknesses and exploit them for everything they have.

This is one of the reasons why such children are afraid of intimacy later on in life. Intimacy requires that you open up to your partner. You have to be vulnerable around one another. You must allow your partner to see you for who you are, with all your weaknesses, embrace you, and love you endlessly.

Exposure to so much hurt while growing up destroys the concept of intimacy for these children. Instead of allowing someone the chance to hurt them, it is easier to cut them off, close all avenues leading to their emotions (Yates, 2010). They crave intimacy like everyone else, but it is so huge a risk. At times the prospect of opening up to intimacy brings back nasty memories, and it is easier to forget about intimacy altogether.

- Affinity for toxic relationships

Toxic relationships are normal for children raised by narcissists. They have a lot of experience in this, and it is easier to embrace these relationships because they almost always know what to expect. They embrace abuse as a normal thing, and that is why they find it easier to entertain people who belittle or envy them.

In early adulthood or later on in life, when they take stock of their friendships and relationships, they realize they have so many toxic people in their lives that they are comfortable around. This happens because they share a bond. The struggle is all too familiar; it is the only thing they know.

- Emotional sabotage

Narcissistic parents create an unhealthy relationship with their children. Children grow up afraid. They know one thing leads to another and are pessimistic about situations. Respect and true love are foreign to them. If they come across someone who loves them unconditionally, it can be unsettling.

What does it even mean to be loved without expecting something back? How does someone even do that? This crisis sets the stage for emotional sabotage. Unconsciously, the child finds a way to sabotage that relationship because it is too good to be real. The defense mechanism for these kids is usually that anything that cannot come too close to them cannot harm them.

It is okay to protect yourself, but at times it comes at a price. Many opportunities are lost, opportunities for learning, growth, careers, and personal intimate relationships.

The following are some of the signs of emotional abuse that you need to be aware of in a relationship with a narcissist:

- Rationalizing the abuse

Abuse in a relationship hurts on so many levels. Victims of narcissists usually end up normalizing the abuse to the point where they deny it happening in the first place. You minimize and rationalize the problem. This is a survival mechanism that helps the victim dissociate from the pain of abuse. You get to a point where you feel your abuser is not a bad person. They had to react the way they did because you probably did something terrible to provoke them.

- Fear of success

Narcissists do not just take away your happiness, they take away your life. At some point, you stop doing the things you used to love. Success becomes a myth for you because it makes you happy, yet your partner hates it when you derive happiness from anything other than themselves. Talent, happiness, joy, and everything else that interests you become a source of darkness, reprimand, and reprisal.

As this continues, you become depressed, lose confidence, anxiety sets in, and you learn to hide away from the spotlight, allowing your partner to shine instead. What your abuser is doing is not keeping you away from your wins because they feel you are not good enough; they do it because they are afraid your success will weaken their hold on you.

- Self-destruction and sabotage

A victim of narcissistic abuse replays the words and actions in their mind all the time until it becomes second nature. You learn to associate certain actions in the relationship with violence and reprimand. You almost expect a negative reaction from your partner each time you do something. This amplification of negativity grows into self-sabotage, and if your partner is a malignant narcissist, suicide might not be so far off.

Chapter 5:

Sexual Abuse

D oes your partner try to force you through words or actions to engage in sexual activity against your will? Does he force himself on you, even when you say "No"? If so, this is a form of harassment and abuse.

If your partner tries to make you (through physical force, threats, insults, guilt trips, etc.) engage in sexual acts that you don't feel comfortable with, this is also sexual harassment and abuse. If any sexual advances are unwanted, and you make it known that they are unwanted and want it to stop, but he or she continues, then it's harassment.

Some abusers assume they have sexual "rights" to their partner, whether or not the partner agrees to the sexual encounter. The abuser cajoles, guilt-trips, shames, or does whatever it takes to coerce or force the victim into sexual activity. This sometimes includes forced sex.

In fact, until 1975, every state in the United States had a "marital exemption" that allowed a husband to rape his wife without fear of legal consequences. Since 1993, all 50 states have enacted laws against marital rape, but, even so, it is still difficult to prove spousal rape.

Please note that spousal or intimate partner rape is a form of physical violence that goes beyond just manipulation and psychological coercion. If sexual harassment has turned into forced sexual acts, please contact the National Domestic Abuse Hotline, law enforcement, or your counselor to get the support you need.

Using sex to manipulate, control, embarrass or shame the person who is supposed to be your most intimate partner is the ultimate act of selfishness and disrespectfulness. It can be one of the most damaging forms of emotional (and physical) abuse. The following are scripts to stop sexual abuse:

Pressuring You to Have Sex

I want you to stop harassing me to have sex. For sex to be enjoyable for me, we need to be in a loving and kind space together. Pressuring and shaming make me want to avoid sex altogether. When you treat me with love, kindness, and respect, that's when I want to have sex with you.

Crossing Your Sexual Boundaries

I do not feel comfortable doing that, and I never will. Stop trying to force or cajole me into doing it now and forever. Respect my boundaries so that we can have a good sex life, or we'll need to go to counseling to figure it out.

Demeaning You During Sex

You may not demean me or make insulting comments about my body during sex. That is deeply unkind and hurtful, and I won't stand for it. I cannot be intimate with someone who speaks this way to me.

Threatening to Cheat on You

Stop threatening to cheat on me when I don't feel like having sex. I am not available to you every moment you want sex. I'm your partner, not just a sexual outlet for you. If you need more sex, we can go to counseling to talk about how to improve our sex life. But threatening affairs will only make things worse between us.

Chapter 6:

Types of Emotional Abuse

O nce you have gotten accustomed to spotting the traits and characteristics of the emotionally abusive person, it will become easy to spot them. You will also start to notice that you feel drained when you are around them. This will help teach you about the different traits, characteristics, and types of emotional abuse.

Psychological abuse can be found everywhere. It can happen amongst friends, at work, in schools, in relationships, and in family life. You can't escape it. These abusers are out there, and it's very hard to avoid them. But it is possible to identify them from the way they act. This is why it is so important to be on the alert and understand how to interpret their actual intentions. These abusive people are also known as toxic people. They are draining and hard to deal with and leave you feeling used.

Scholars and psychologists aren't totally sure how to evaluate them because these abusers are far from suffering from a mental illness. In the majority of cases, they create damage by using the power they have over others.

There are many red flags to help warn you and make sure that you don't get trapped by another emotionally abusive person. The first things we are going to look at are these warnings.

Parental Abuse

This is probably a type of abuse that you don't want to think about, but it happens and is fairly common. This can include abuse from stepparents, guardians, grandparents, and anybody else that is a parental figure in a child's life. Here's an example: Grandma Jean came to visit and made some comments about her granddaughter, how fat she was looking, and how she dresses. While the comments are infrequent and it might not seem like abuse at first, the derogatory statements are abuse. Grandma isn't doing much to help the child gain confidence; instead, she is taking it away from her.

Hurtful and offhanded comments, like the ones from the example, are just one instance where abuse doesn't actually require a pattern from a single person. Children tend to be more sensitive to things like this, and such comments leave a lasting impression when they happen over a long period of time and on a regular basis. In fact, the more people say certain things to a child, the more they are affected.

Constant negative comments aimed towards different personality traits from physical appearance to behavior have a lasting impression on a child. While it's sad how frequently this abuse happens between parents and children, what's worse is the complicated reason behind the abuse. Parents who berate their children with the reason for causing harm are disturbed people. Chances are, though, the parent doesn't actually hate their child. Their hurtful remarks are likely due to incompetence.

For example, if a child is a little heavier or they have developed a few unhealthy habits, their parent's comments could be their warped way of expressing their concern about their wellbeing. This is ineffective and harmful, but, unfortunately, harshness and insults are the only things that some people understand. There's actually a good chance that the parents were raised with these types of insults as well.

This likely has you all wondering where parenting fits into things. Where is the line drawn between abuse and a strict parent? First off, discipline is important in a child's life. The right kind of discipline can create a strong character and teach right from wrong. To positively discipline a child, you have to teach them to respect rules and have strong values, a sense of morality, and a strong work ethic. Well-disciplined children are safer in the world as adults.

For some parents, strict parenting means creating a rigid daily routine for all their activities. Providing a child with a no-budge schedule is most often considered strict, but it isn't abuse. Discipline becomes abusive when the consequences and punishment from infractions turn inconsistent, excessive, and focus on causing fear instead of teaching them valuable lessons.

Abusive parents won't think much about how they discipline their child, and the punishments that they inflict will often be on a whim. Rather than explaining what they did wrong, the punishments are outbursts and little more than psychological torture or deprivation. The most common feature of an abusive home environment is unpredictability.

Relationship Abuse

Emotional abuse happens a lot between parent and child, but it also happens in other relationships with friends, spouses, or boyfriend/girlfriend. Most of the time, the person being abused isn't new to it. They likely faced emotional abuse as a child.

Let's not forget that men can be victims as well. TV, movies, social media, and the like seem to put emphasis on women being abused. It's important to make sure women get help, but something we don't see a lot of is how men are susceptible to being emotionally abused. Society has conditioned us to believe that men are always strong and never bullied, but it happens more than we think.

The problem is, though, a man being emotionally abused by a woman is more stigmatized than physical abuse. This is why most men won't report psychological terror.

Female-specific spousal abuse isn't all that different from male-specific. The one thing women tend to do more than a man is use sex as a weapon of control. In some extreme cases, the woman might threaten the man with accusations of rape.

I'm by no means trying to lessen what women face; I just want to shed some light on the other side of the story. When this type of abuse starts in a marriage, it tends to begin with one spouse trying to make things easier, and this causes them to isolate themselves.

Besides the common forms of control, men are more capable of causing specific types of emotional abuse. This is especially true for inflicting fear and threats of violence.

Both men and women, when abusive, will belittle, humiliate and withhold affection from their partner. They try to control the relationships their partners have outside of the marriage as well. This type of behavior can last for years. Only when one spouse moves on or is pushed too far, do they realize that trauma has taken place.

The most common cause of spousal abuse is a broken home. This isn't true for all, but it is common. The abuse is not your fault, and an important step in healing is to instill this truth in your mind. It's easy to become complacent, to just accept what is going on, and believe you can't do anything to change it, but you can stop it and heal.

Now, marriage isn't the only place emotional abuse can happen. It can occur in any relationship. This tends to be harder to notice, but then something changes within the relationship.

When it comes to abusive friendships, a lot of people underestimate how damaging the abuse can be. This is because friendships are viewed as things that can be easily disposed of, more so than marriages. True friends are not that common anymore and have turned into a wide circle of acquaintances. This means that friendships can be easily found but take years to build.

This is what makes misinterpreting an abusive friendship for a true friend so dangerous. The need for a friend causes a blind spot and leaves you holding onto a person who is only interested in using you for personal gain. They are nice when they need something, but it changes when you become less useful. This type of tainted friendship can happen to anybody, especially those who are considered "social butterflies."

Just because you may not be socially active doesn't mean that you have to settle for a person who belittles you and calls you names. Plus, it's a truth of life that it is better to be alone than be with a person who abuses you. This might sound harsh, but you'll find more success once you stop allowing yourself to be used by others who don't care about you. You will then start to attract those who actually care.

Rejecting

A common trait of emotionally abusive people is rejecting their victim. A partner, parent, friend, or caregiver who displaces this type of behavior toward another will let their victim know, in different ways, that they aren't wanted. Belittling a person or putting down their worth are some ways that this type of emotional abuse manifests. Other types of rejecting can include telling a person to leave or, worse, calling them names, making them a scapegoat, or blaming them for other people's problems. Refusing to hold a child as they are growing or refusing to talk to another person are also abusive behaviors.

Ignoring

Adults who haven't really had their emotional needs met will find it hard to respond to the needs of others, especially their own children. They may not be able to attach to others or provide a positive nurturing experience for their child. They might not show any interest in a person, or they withhold affection, or might not even acknowledge that another person is present. They are likely physically there but are completely emotionally unavailable. Failing to respond to another is emotional abuse.

Terrorizing

People who curse, yell, and threaten their child, spouse, or friend are doing serious psychological damage. Now, we talked about yelling earlier. Yelling and cursing are fine if it is temporary and the cause of it is addressed, and you have a healthy conversation about what made them upset. Cursing and yelling at another person constantly or for no reason is where it becomes abuse.

Singling out a person and ridiculing them for normal emotional reactions is abusive. Threatening a person with abandonment, physical harm, harsh words, or in severe cases, death is completely unacceptable. Even if you are joking, causing a person to be terrified by intimidation or threats is some of the worst emotional abuse. When it comes to children, this includes knowing, hearing, or witnessing abuse within the home.

Isolating

This is a common abuse tactic by parents. When parents use isolation, they may not let their children engage in normal activities with their peers. They may keep a baby in their room, unexposed to external stimulation, or they can prevent their teen from participating in extracurricular activities. Requiring somebody to stay in their room from the time they get home from school until they go to school the next day, restricting what they eat, or forcing them to stay away from friends and family can be very destructive, depending on the severity and circumstances.

Corrupting

People who are corruptive to others may allow their child to partake in drugs or alcohol or may enable the user. They talk others into treating animals cruelly or participate in criminal activities like gambling, prostitution, assault, stealing, and so on. Abusive parents might let their children watch inappropriate content for their age. Encouraging others to do things that are harmful or illegal is abusive and needs to be reported.

Chapter 7:

Abusive Relationship vs. Healthy Relationship

E very relationship is different - each one has its own beauty, as well as its own imperfections. Since the dawn of mankind, human beings have survived and thrived due to social companionship - whether those are through tribes, communities, families, or partners.

It is in our nature to seek companionship to feel safe and fulfilled, and romantic relationships are often the most sought out form of companionship. People usually crave having someone to share things with and to grow old with; knowing they have someone in their corner.

The basis of being in a relationship is usually to find true love, a great friend, and happiness. However, like most things in life, relationships also come with their own challenges. Even though a relationship entails two souls coming together to care for each other and love each other, these souls are still individual people with their own personalities, core values, and beliefs.

No matter how similar or different these two people are, the way they conduct and maintain their relationship will determine whether or not it is a healthy one.

It is sometimes confusing to know whether the relationship you are in is, in fact, healthy or not. Each person has their own preferences, tolerances, vices, etc.

Who is to say what the universal definition of a happy relationship is? While the meaning of a happy relationship may differ from person to person, there are several universal truths that determine whether your relationship is healthy or unhealthy:

Being Content Within Yourself

For one to achieve a healthy relationship, you need to have a healthy relationship with yourself first. This means loving yourself unconditionally and feeling whole. It all starts with you.

We are constantly growing and changing, but before we get into a relationship with somebody, we should know who we are, what we want from life, and what we want in a relationship.

We should feel confident about ourselves and be willing to be our authentic selves with another person. Being content with yourself means being able to validate yourself instead of seeking validation from someone else.

If you aren't whole and happy with yourself, your glass is only half full. If two people come together expecting the other person to fill up their glass, they may be disappointed, as the other person may not have that much to give from their glass either.

This can turn into an unhealthy codependent relationship that exhausts both parties.

Understanding What True Love Actually Looks Like

Love is a concept that many of us wish to bring to life but may not fully understand. We might think we know what true love is based on past relationships, romance movies, and novels, or simply from what people tell us. What true love actually is, is a choice. It is the choice we make to love someone wholeheartedly every day. While love is based on emotion, a choice is based on logic and reason. It is easy to fall in love with someone quickly because your emotions take over, and you are addicted to that temporary feeling of happiness. However, once the romance and honeymoon period fades, which it will, true love will be determined by your CHOICE to keep loving this person through thick and thin. A choice based on reason and logic.

If we can choose to remain close to our best friends, we can apply the same principle to our relationships - we can choose to love them every day, come what may. No relationship will constantly be magical and perfect; there will be times when you really question whether you want to keep going. At those times, the relationships that survive are the ones that are built from two people choosing to truly love each other every day regardless. True love is when two people consciously know everything about each other (the good and the bad) and still choose to love each other and be with each other. Of course, this does not mean that you forgive your partner for abusive behavior and choose to stay with them regardless of how they treat you. True love also means respecting each other, and if you are not being respected, then your relationship is probably not very healthy.

If you ever asked an elderly couple what kept them together all these years, they would probably say it is acceptance and understanding. They have made the decision to be with each other, taking into consideration every single aspect of the other person. They have accepted who their partner is and understand the way they operate. Only when you are able to accept and understand the other person

51

are you able to use your logical reasoning to decide whether you want to be with this person. Paradoxically, logic is what makes your love true and pure.

Accepting Your Partner for Who They Truly Are

Healthy relationships involve two people loving each other wholeheartedly, which means that they also accept each other for the way they are.

The first step is to accept yourself, flaws and all. Self-love is the key to having a healthy relationship with someone else. If you are able to accept yourself, you can be content within yourself.

When you are content from within, you are capable of accepting your partner for the way they are and will not expect them to change either.

Of course, if there are tiny aspects about your partner (or about you) that can be discussed and changed for the betterment of the relationship, that is totally understandable and healthy.

However, if you are unhappy with who your partner is at their very core, in terms of their values, beliefs, and personality, you are going to have an unhappy relationship because you will constantly try to change them.

This can lead to consistent disappointment and feeling short-changed, while your partner could feel resentment towards you and insecure with themselves.

If you truly love someone for who they are, you would not want to change them. It is as simple as that.

Being Honest and Respectful

This goes without saying - honesty and respect are extremely vital in a healthy relationship. When you and your partner are able to be completely honest with each other and respect each other in every way, only then will your relationship make you feel secure and happy. When you both are honest with each other, you are coming from a place of emotional maturity. There will be times when the truth may not be something neither of you wants to hear, but the fact that it is being laid out shows that you respect each other and you want what is best for the other person.

Open communication is essential to making your relationship work, and if honesty is met with an emotional reaction, that may harm your relationship more than help. When someone is being honest with you, they are taking a big step and letting you in on the truth, even when it hurts. By doing this, they are respecting you enough to make sure you are not in the dark, oblivious to the truth. They believe that you are able to handle the truth and are able to tell you anything. At this point, it is best to show that person respect rather than react with emotion because they are taking a big step by being honest.

In emotionally abusive relationships, when the abuser is feeling insecure or reacts with emotion, they exhibit defensiveness to the person being honest, and this usually results in a conflict, as they perceive this honesty to be an attack on their character. These kinds of arguments are based solely on insecurity and emotional reaction when the conversation should be a healthy conversation about what was said. The more someone reacts to honesty rather than listens, the less their partner will be inclined to be honest in the future, as they will gravitate towards avoiding conflict. This is where relationships become toxic and unhealthy, as couples start to hide things from each other. Thus, it is important that partners respect each other and take a few breaths before responding to whatever is being said so that a productive and positive conversation can take place.

There Should Be Mutual Trust

If you do not trust each other, then you do not have a healthy relationship. Being committed to someone means sharing a big part of your life with this person. Aspects of your life become intertwined, and this person becomes extremely important to you.

If you do not trust them, either because of their character or because of emotional wounds, you may have yet to heal, that could lead to a lot of pain. If you get anxious when your partner goes out with their friends without you, or you check their phone regularly, then you have low levels of trust in your partner.

Mutual trust brings partners closer together, as both of you feel secure and safe with the other person. If this is not the case, you both can try to build your trust for the other. However, this only works if both partners are willing to work at it and be understanding of the other person's vulnerabilities.

Taking Responsibility for Your Own Feelings

Your partner will most likely push your buttons, and it is important to recognize when this happens. In a healthy relationship, you should be able to take responsibility for what you are thinking and how you feel because you and only you are in charge of how you react to situations. For example, if your partner hurls a hurtful comment at you and you get upset, the first step is to recognize that getting upset is the reaction you chose to have. It is okay to feel what you feel, but from there, it is vital to think about what you can do to relieve that emotion or thought - whether it is taking some space to cool off or talking to your partner about it in a constructive manner.

Unhealthy relationships involve the person who has been hurt blaming their partner for their feelings. Their partner may be the trigger or the situation that caused them to have a reaction, but they did not dictate how the person should have felt, and vice versa. The person is choosing to feel this way and also choosing whether they want to stew in that feeling or to find a way to resolve it and let it go. It's not the easiest thing to do, but with practice, it becomes an automatic behavior.

Chapter 8:

How to Leave an Abusive Relationship?

O ne of the things that you have to realize is that a narcissist does not see the need to seek help from a therapist because, after all, they think that there is nothing wrong with them. Recovery is for those who have been through abuse. If you have been or are in a relationship with a narcissist, it is high time you left and sought help from a professional. It is this kind of support that you need to rebuild your self-confidence and bounce back to your self-esteem.

Trust me; you are better than you have ever thought possible. The narcissist might have managed to puncture your self-confidence and even crushed your self-esteem, but most importantly, you are just a victim. You are not unworthy like they want you to believe. Finding a health professional with a specialty in trauma recovery will help you journey through the healing process to recovery. If you are not able to leave the relationship, a therapist can also help you to learn the best ways in which you can communicate effectively with your abuser so that you can set boundaries that they will respect and hence, protect you so that they will no longer take advantage of you.

Here are some of the steps that you will have to go through to help you journey through healing to recovery:

Step 1: Cut Contact

Once you have left the relationship, keep it at that! Stop maintaining contact with your abuser. The main reason why you left is that the situation was not working for you. Therefore, there is nothing that will happen that can make things better. The best way to recover from abuse is for you to block all forms of communication.

If you have joint custody of children, you may not be able to wipe this person entirely from your life. It is therefore advisable to create a strict custom contract, according to which you only communicate on matters regarding your children using third-party channels exclusively! Otherwise, ensure that you have set up court orders for all forms of agreements.

Think about the extreme trauma bonding, the gross abuse, and the addiction you had to the narcissist. Sometimes the best way is for you to accept that the only way you can recover from such damage is to pull away and cut your losses once and for all. Think of abstaining as a way of protecting yourself from hurt. In other words, each time you initiate contact with your abuser, you are handing them the ammunition to blow you off.

Remember that you lived with them, and so they know what your weak points are and how they can wound you even more profoundly. It is not until we heal that we will stop forcing ourselves on the narcissist for love or craving them or even justifying to ourselves giving them a second chance. When we completely stop contact, then we can begin to heal.

Step 2: Release That Trauma So That You Begin Functioning Again

If we are going to heal, we have to be willing to reclaim our power. We have to do the exact opposite of what we used to believe; 'I can fix him/her, I will feel better.' Your power belongs inside you. The moment you take your focus away from your abuser, you will be able to channel that power into rebuilding your self-love and paying closer attention to making yourself whole again.

At first, it might seem like understanding who a narcissist is and what they do is essential. But the real truth is that these things cannot heal your internal trauma. What you need to do is to decide to let go of that horrific experience so that you can be at peace. You will begin to rise, get relief, and feel balanced again once you have decided to take your power where it belongs—inside you.

Step 3: Forgive Yourself For What You Have Been Through

When the insecure and wounded parts of us are still in pain, we often are pushed into behaving like children who are damaged. We often look for people's approval, and especially from our abuser, we hand our abuser the power to treat us as they see fit. And that's the time you realize that you have given them all your resources: money, time, and health. The most unfortunate thing is that while doing that, you end up hurting the people that matter the most in your life... your children, siblings, parents, and friends.

Yes, it might be hard to forgive yourself for this, but you can do that if you want to rebuild your life and everything you lost to your abuser. By working through your healing process, you will soon find resolution and acceptance. You can move away from lacking self-love and respect to living a life full of truth and responsibility, and well-being.

You will realize that when you forgive yourself, you acknowledge that this was all a learning curve, and this is the experience you learned, and hence, you will use that to reclaim your life. It is when you release your regrets and self-judgments that you can start setting yourself free to realize greatness in your life irrespective of what stage you are at. This is the point when you will begin to feel hope again, hope that will steer you forward into fulfillment and a life full of purpose.

Step 4: Release Everything And Heal All Your Fears Of The Abuser And What They Might Do Next

Do you know what bait to a narcissist is? -Anxiety, pain, and distress. These are the things that can perpetuate another cycle of abuse no matter how we tell ourselves that we have separated from them. It is indeed true that abusers can be relentless. In most cases, they do not like being losers. But one thing that you have to understand is that they are not as powerful and impactful as you may have thought them to be.

They need you to fear and go through pain so that they can function. Once you have healed your emotional trauma, they fall apart. Therefore, it is crucial that you become grounded and stoic by not feeding into their drama; this way, they will soon wither away along with their power and credibility.

Step 5: Release The Connection To Your Abuser

So many people have likened their freedom from a narcissist to that of exorcism. When we liberate ourselves from the darkness that filled our beings, we allow ourselves to detox and let light and life come in. If that light has to take over the shade, the darkness has to leave so that there is space for something new to come in. In the same manner, it is essential that you release all the parts that were trapped by your abuser so that you can tap into a more supernatural power, the power of pure creativity.

When you disentangle yourself from the narcissist, it is not just about cutting the cord; it is also about releasing all the belief systems you might have associated yourself with subconsciously. It is only then that you can break free to be a new person and not a target of a narcissist.

Even though it might be tempting to seek revenge on your abuser, this is something that you have to try hard to avoid. Rage has the power of pulling you back into deeper darkness and a game that your abuser is an expert at in the first place. The best form of revenge is one in which you decide to take back your freedom and render your abuser irrelevant.

And it is likely going to crush their ego, and they will be powerless and at a loss that they cannot even affect you. Often they are in despair when it hits that you are a constant reminder of their extinction. It is at this point that the cycle ends, and your soul contracts to allow love and healing in so that you can be whole again.

Step 6: Realize Your Liberation, Truth, And Freedom

Traditionally, we learn that loving ourselves is a very selfish act. However, when it comes to finding liberation and freedom from the hands of our abusers, it is a very critical step that allows us to take in the truth and let it set us free from captivity. Yes, it is something incredibly difficult to do, but it is a necessary step toward achieving liberation.

Society has taught us that we are treated by others the same way we treat them. However, this is a false premise because we get treatment according to the way we treat ourselves. In other words, the measure of love that we get from others is equivalent to what we feel about ourselves.

Therefore, when we open up to healing and recovery, we open the doors for others to love us in reality and in more healthy ways than ever before. It is this act that serves as a template by which we teach our children so that they do not carry around subconscious patterns of abuse that were passed to us. This positive modeling only starts when we decide to take responsibility for our happiness and freedom. We slowly become the change that we would wish to see so that we can let go of being someone's victim and stop handing other people our power.

In other words, we take back our lives by doing everything necessary to aid our inner healing irrespective of what the narcissist does or does not do, something that's now irrelevant either way. It is at this point that we can thrive despite what we have been through and what has happened to us.

So, What Do You Need To Learn?

Refocus

One of the best things that you need to learn from the whole experience is the dangers that are associated with holding on to emotional attachments. It is when you let go that you will be able to experience the power that comes with healing. Take time to release the bonds to your abuser so that you can refocus all of your efforts on building yourself and a new life.

Self-confidence

If you are going to live a life of greatness after your abuse, you have to be willing to start putting back your life together. You have to come out with self-confidence so that you can reclaim your old self and find an even higher power to steer you forward towards success and victory. Once you start experiencing self-love, it is then that you will be able to turn a chaotic life into one that has calmness and joy.

Mindfulness

One of the things that you need to learn is to be fully present in the moment. This is where your mind is not anxious about anything. It's the moment when you are calm and have clarity of thought and thought process. It is only then that you can learn some of the powerful tools and tricks that can bring you instantly to the present so that you can live a life full of purpose and adventure.

Chapter 9:

What Happens After Leaving an Abusive Relationship

Although being with a narcissist is a truly horrific and often traumatic experience, breaking free can lead to initial loneliness. You are so used to being with that person, being involved in their stories, games, and sense of companionship, even if it is a twisted and mentally- emotionally abusive companionship; that finally leaving and being free can leave you feeling empty. This is natural- we are all chalices waiting to be filled. We need connections, stories, relationships, and various realities to keep us feeling alive and fulfilled. So when you break free from the narcissist, you are essentially an empty vessel. What new stories are you going to create?

This is, of course, in itself a beautiful process and fundamentally part of your journey. To be alone is to be all one, content, free, and soulfully happy in your own independence. Once we remove attachments and stories which are no longer good for us, we provide ourselves the space and time for new stories, new realities, and frequencies of being. I once heard the saying that life is like music. Life can be equated with music. We do live in a universe, after all! So, loneliness can be overcome by filling yourself with new stories- ones in harmony with your best interests and the best possible expression of you.

Connected to this are a self-recovery, healing, and boundary plan. Boundaries are very important, but so is your personal re-discovery of self and self-healing. Below are five key and highly effective ways to overcome loneliness.

Passion Projects

Immerse yourself in a passion project. New hobbies, favorite pastimes, or creating a vision board to align with your dreams and aspirations can all be marvelous gateways back to your true self. Following your greatest joy allows you to overcome loneliness and heal from the sufferings caused by your narcissistic partner. Passion and fire are the sparks of life; they re-energize and revitalize your inner core, further enabling you to stop feeling isolated or cut off from the world. This is an unfortunate consequence of being the victim of narcissistic abuse or mind manipulation—you may feel disconnected from others on a profound level. Refinding yourself through a passion project is essential for your well-being.

Re-Finding Yourself ("Know Thyself!")

Have you ever heard of the saying "know thyself"? This is knowing yourself on every level; your intentions, goals, dreams, hidden motivations, and your personality in its entirety. We usually become lost and allow in the illusions and judgments of others when we do not know ourselves. 'The self' is the holistic part of being, the persona, characteristics, and beliefs that make us unique. It is our thoughts, feelings, subtle impressions, emotions, past experience, and deeper inner workings, also having a soulful aspect or significance. Recovering from a narcissist and refinding yourself tie in closely to knowing yourself or knowing thyself. Not only can taking steps to rediscover and know thyself help you overcome loneliness, but it will also help increase your self-esteem, self-worth, and personal confidence.

Meditation

As briefly delved into earlier, meditation is one of the most profound ways to heal from a narcissist. Feeling lonely is due to feelings of separation or disconnectedness, and these all stem from your mind and emotions. Meditating reconnects you to your true self, inner harmony, and a sense of peace and well-being. It also expands your mind and allows you to be an observer of any chaotic, destructive, or afflictive thoughts, beliefs, or emotions. During the many months or years of narcissistic abuse, you will have been through some terrible, manipulative treatment. You may have been gaslighted, made to feel small, weak or inferior, or generally insulted on repeat. Your feelings, opinions, and perspectives may have been overlooked, and where your beautiful qualities and strengths should have been supported, encouraged, and cherished, you instead received neglect and abuse. All in all, your partner knocked your confidence and self-esteem in many unseen ways.

These all have profound negative effects on your inner belief systems, psyche, and unconscious workings. Thoughts and emotions, which shape and define you as a person, are strongly influenced by experience and memories; so any abuse you may have suffered can become deeply ingrained. Meditation fills you with a "conscious emptiness," an empty space for new levels of thought, feeling, and awareness. You may be able to access your higher self and higher mind, feel better and more positive about your life, and see all negative happenings as an opportunity for growth and new wisdom. In short, feeling lonely is replaced with feeling empowered.

Self-Therapy

The importance and power of self-therapy really cannot be undermined or overlooked. Self-therapy is any type of therapy that can be performed at home or in our own time. It is great for the mind, body, emotions, and spirit. It is not just your thoughts and emotions which suffer during narcissistic abuse but also your soul, the core and hidden part of yourself. This is the part that allows us to feel love, empathy, a deeper connection to others and life's beauty; connect with music and access transcendental states, and develop advanced cognitive, intuitive, and emotional frequency functioning.

Self-therapy incorporates a wide range of choices and channels, so, fortunately, there is bound to be at least one route that works for you. Meditation, sound therapy, nature therapy, music, art, creative expression, spiritual literature, yoga, tai chi, massage, energy work, and mindfulness are all forms of self-therapy. In fact, many people can change their whole mindset through the self-love and care which comes with engaging in therapy. Choosing to give yourself a healing massage, listening to soothing and peaceful music, and going for a mindful walk in nature, or reading some soulful poetry can all be effective self-therapies in their own rights.

New Social Groups and Organizations

Balanced with all the other key ways to overcome loneliness and heal for the long term is the engagement of new social groups and organizations. This can include peer support, groups for victims of narcissistic abuse, or simply any organization or venture which allows you to feel good. Being happy and connecting with others is the best way to let go and move forward with your life, despite the initial loneliness you may feel. You can feel lonely or isolated in a group too, because the truth is loneliness is just a mindset. Some people feel lonely even when surrounded by family and peers, just as many feel most at peace and blissful when alone. True happiness and contentment come from your ability to connect and feel at ease with the world. Taking the first steps by putting yourself out there will re-spark your passion for life and connection and your connection with yourself.

Boundaries: Your New Power Word

Boundaries are your new power word! Breaking free and liberating yourself cannot occur until you put healthy boundaries in place. Not only do they need to be healthy, but they need to be strong, so there is no chance of magnetizing or attracting another narcissistic relationship into your orbit.

Let's look at all the ways to create, develop and maintain a boundary plan.

1. Positive Self-Talk and Power Words

Positive self-talk may not initially appear as a form of boundary creation; however, it is. Self-talk is the conversations we have with ourselves. When we engage in positive self-talk, we open new neural pathways and actively influence the neurons in our brains. These neurons are responsible for how we think, feel, and respond to people, situations, and experiences. They are also responsible for our communication, both internal, with ourselves, and external, through our interactions with others. Just through positive and mindful self-talk, a natural boundary is created due to the ripple effect thoughts have on inner and external reality. In short, an invisible energy field is created through the power of the mind, thoughts, and subtle intentions exhibited. This invisible energy field is your boundaries.

Connected to this is the effect of power words, specific words used with self-talk to enhance and amplify the power of your boundaries. Words can, in fact, be used, spoken, or thought like a mantra or affirmation for optimum effect. Neuroscientists have discovered the incredible influence thoughts have on our physical being, emotions, and overall well-being or vibratory state (inner frequency), and this is backed up by a number of other schools of thought. Neuro-linguistic programming, cognitive behavioral therapy, and many alternative therapies and healing modalities all recognize and support the truth that our thoughts are powerful shapers and creators of our world. It is not only inner currents that are affected but worldly reality as we know it. So, harnessing the power of your mind in your boundary goals will allow your personal boundaries to expand and grow stronger, assisting you for the better.

2. Self-Affirmations

Connected to this are self-affirmations or affirmations. Self-affirmations are essentially affirmations that can be spoken or thought during meditation or any contemplative activity for great effect. They are best performed as a sort of ritual or daily integrated habit. Taking time to dedicate some minutes to affirmations daily will enable your aura, your electromagnetic energy field to be strengthened and expanded, and your mind strengthened. As the body is a complex and interconnected system, this has a profound effect on your emotions and thus increases your sense of boundaries on many levels. Mental boundaries, emotional boundaries, physical boundaries, and spiritual boundaries are real, and once you begin to truly develop your own boundaries, you will realize how 'one and the same' these all are. Once you strengthen one of your boundaries, you can protect yourself from harmful or destructive energy. This includes the intentions and attempted projections of your narcissistic ex!

To engage in self-affirmations effectively, make time for a daily morning and/ or evening routine. This routine creates a structure in your life and an almost 'ceremonial' aspect. This is precisely what affirmations are, a sort of ceremony-like meditation. Setting your intentions and committing to self-affirmations as a daily routine inevitably sharpens and strengthens your mind, further opening you up to new ways of perceiving. Included in this is protecting yourself and the connection this morning or evening routine has to self-healing and strengthening your aura.

3. Self-Healing/ Aura Strengthening

Kirlian photography has shown how there is an electromagnetic energy field surrounding each one us known as an aura to some. Spiritual beings, healers, and energy workers have been aware of this energy field or aura for quite some time; however, it is only in recent years that the science to support it has made itself known. All living entities have an electromagnetic energy field, from plants to animals and homo sapiens. This energy field is responsible for all thoughts, feelings, subtle impressions, beliefs, interactions, emotions, past memories and experiences, and one's general energy and vibration. We give off vibrations in every moment, and this is where the modern age term "vibes" has originated from. In terms of Kirlian photography, one's aura can be seen to show just how real subtle energy and influences are.

Chapter 10:

How Can I Recover from the Emotional and Mental Wounds Left by the Abuser?

N arcissists are opportunistic hunters. They will target whoever is in reach, but they prefer to seek out a challenge. When the intended victim is someone who is more settled in their own sense of self and is confident, outgoing, and spontaneous, they will present an even more tempting target to the pathological narcissist. Dodgson (2018) indicates that narcissists enjoy the challenge of taking down someone who will provide them with some resistance. It doesn't really thrill them to take power from a weak person; instead, they enjoy the thrill of taking down someone who is also dominant and strong. So, if you are the target of a narcissist or you have become their victim, do not doubt yourself and say it is because you are/were weak. Instead, you should focus on the road to recovery once you have left the narcissist or have escaped from the abuse.

Even narcissists who only occasionally gaslight you or only abuse you to a lesser extent can inflict some pretty horrific and long-lasting damage. You can't simply go on with your life and hope to heal. Chances are that you are damaged in ways that you are not even aware of yet, or if you are aware of how much the abuse has affected you, you may be too lost to find the road forward. In both these cases, you need a strategy or "a street guide" to help you find your way.

In planning your road to recovery, you may need to formulate a strategy–just like in chess–to help you cope and help you back onto your feet. Otherwise, you will remain the gaslighter's pawn long after they have left your life.

Why We Fall Victim

According to Dodgson (2018), narcissists enjoy targeting people who match their own perfect ideal; hence, they will go for strong individuals, especially people who take care of themselves on an external level. They may be attracted to beautiful, well-groomed, physically fit individuals. At first, they may see these people as their perfect partner or friend. However, that sadly does not remain the case, and they will systematically drain you of your power and what had at first attracted them to you until you are so torn down that you no longer appeal to them and then get discarded.

Empathically strong people are also prime targets for narcissists since they make the narcissist feel good by sharing their understanding with them. Narcissists thrive on people who try to help them. Karen Arluck, a psychotherapist (Dodgson, 2018), believes that narcissists target:

- People who are in some way impressive or admired
- People who compliment them or try to help them
- People who fit their perfect ideal
- People who validate them, try to understand them, and will not be likely to leave or quit on them

Contrary to popular belief, narcissistic abusers tend to go for strong people, not emotionally frail people (Dodgson, 2019).

Future Strategies

Narcissists want to drive you crazy with doubt and fear. They gaslight you to make you doubt your own grasp on reality. By developing an action plan and sticking to it, you can be prepared for future assaults by your abuser. When drawing up your action plan, you may want to consider the following areas to plan for:

- Set boundaries

It is important to know what you will ignore, what you will accept, and what you need to avoid. A colleague, who is a little self-centered and makes the occasional jab at you to bolster their own self-esteem, may fall into the "ignore" category; however, a colleague who engages in sexual harassment and then makes you feel like you started it or that you liked it, would definitely fall in the "avoid" category. Do not accept this form of abuse. Once you have set your boundaries, stick to them.

- Know your rights

Whether the abuse happens at home, at work, or in a social setting, you have rights. Know them. In most democracies, the rights set out in the Universal Declaration of Human Rights of 1948 apply. Interestingly, these rights were drafted due to the merciless and inhuman acts perpetrated by Hitler (a historical narcissist) during World War II. The following are rights that may be infringed upon by a narcissistic abuser, and you can use the powers of the law against such abuse:

- o The right to say no to sex

- o The right to privacy

- o The right to be respected (to not be shouted at, not humiliated, or victimized)

- o The right to dignity

- o The right to safety and peace of mind

If you are suffering a violation of your basic human rights, you can seek legal representation and should know that you are protected by the law.

- Create consequences

Lancer (2018) writes that we need to set consequences that match violations of our boundaries. This is crucial since it can give you an instant way to act, instead of overthinking and then becoming confused and then overreacting. Just like the prior, long-winded sentence, which sort of loses the plot, you need to avoid an emotional run-on and the jumbled reactions that this creates.

- Support

Develop the guts to ask a friend that you trust to be your soundboard. In using an objective person to talk to about the manipulative patterns that the abuser is creating in your life, you can develop the ability to see their schemes and manipulations. Beware the isolation habits that narcissists and other emotional abusers perpetuate. They want to keep their victim all to themselves. You need to find supportive friends who can help to keep your mind in order.

Staik (2019) writes that people who repel narcissists are individuals who are supremely confident in themselves, and they leave no gap where doubt may creep in that may be exploited by the narcissist. They can see that the gaslighting is really about the narcissist and not about them. This allows them to avoid getting emotionally hurt by investing their emotions in themselves and not in the narcissist. They quickly let the narcissist know that they know what the abuser is doing. Remember that narcissists work on the sly, and once they are told (in no uncertain terms) that you know what they are up to, they lose interest in you since they know they will not accomplish anything.

To work effectively on your own recovery, you need to go beyond simply looking at the future (though this is essential too), and you need to heal the hurts you already have. Here's how.

- Forgiveness and Letting Go

Many victims of narcissistic abuse struggle to get back on their feet. They blame themselves for not seeing the manipulations of their abuser for what it really was—abuse. Inner Integration (2018) writes that this may have a lot to do with you suffering the effects of Stockholm Syndrome, where you identify more with your abuser than with yourself. You end up making excuses for the abuser, who holds such a central role in your life, and as a result, you feel like you were responsible for the abuse. To move on after the abuse has ended, you may need to first forgive yourself for any perceived "flaws" on your part. Affirmations are a great way to do this. If you begin to listen to your own thoughts, you may begin to hear echoes of your abuser's voice, and it is up to you to counter their voice and reclaim your own identity.

Here are some affirmations that may prove beneficial:

- "I am strong enough to move forward."

- "I forgive myself for caring about someone who did not deserve it."

- "I can love people who treat me with love and respect."

- "It is okay to say "No" to someone who does not have my best interests at heart."

In extreme cases, your emotional damage may have manifested biologically, actually changing the make-up of your brain chemistry. Indeed, it is quite possible to exhaust your feel-good chemical neurotransmitters like serotonin and dopamine. In these cases, you may require medical intervention, and this is not something to be ashamed of. It is not another way that you fall short—it is you taking care of your body and mind and acting responsibly.

If you do not forgive yourself for your role in an abusive relationship, you will not be able to move forward or let go. You need to face the fact that you made mistakes and that it is okay.

Forgiving yourself is about you letting go of your flaws and embracing your own life. It is essential that you make peace with yourself following an abusive episode so that you can move forward and let go of the negative effects of the abuse.

Sometimes you will need to face the reality that you may need to forgive yourself and your abuser to move forward. Remember that forgiveness is not the same as saying that it is okay. By forgiving your abuser, you are not giving them permission to inflict more abuse. Rather, it is you saying that you are now letting them go so that you no longer suffer continued abuse at their hands and at the memories of their abuse. This is how you let go.

Inner Integration (2018) also writes that for victims who repeatedly fall into the abuse cycle, they may need to delve deeper into their lives and find the original abuse that they suffered. Most often, the patterns of abuse started in childhood, and if you do not take ownership of that abuse and heal that wound, you will repeatedly fall back under a narcissist's spell.

Chapter 11:

What Are Some Ways to Heal Yourself After Having Experienced Emotional Abuse?

When you have emotional trauma, it becomes difficult for you to control your emotions. When in this state, the trauma survivor is left vulnerable that the slightest physical, sensory, and emotional cues cause panic as it reminds them of the abuse and trauma.

During this time, the body and mind activate the same way as if exposed to an existing threat. It feels confusing and terrifying to the trauma survivors when they experience this. Learning some grounding and self-soothing techniques help to regulate the emotions when panic sets in.

When you try these techniques, you can feel safer now as it enhances your calm state.

Benefits of Grounding Techniques

When you feel intense anxiety or emotions threaten to overwhelm you, grounding techniques help you remain in the present moment. Doing this will allow you to feel in control and know that you are safe, not back to the abuse.

Staying in the moment means you must focus on the physical world and the sensations you feel right now. You can use these skills whenever your emotions are wild or distressed after your emotions were triggered. During this situation, you become stressed by being caught up with the problematic thoughts and memories of your past encounters with the narcissist.

Reliving bad experiences can make you feel afraid, leading to the development of negative habits. Some of those habits include drinking, binge eating, sleeping, and addictions. These are opposites of healing, which you can prevent from happening through grounding techniques.

How to Do a Grounding Technique

It is easy to perform a grounding technique. When you feel panic or overwhelming emotions, focus on an aspect or sensation of the physical world. For instance, touch the ground or hold the hands of your friend. The impressions you get from these will focus on the internal thoughts and feelings that plague your mind.

When it comes to grounding techniques, you must always practice. Doing this helps you calm down naturally after getting upset. When performing your grounding skills, you must focus on the external experience or the outward appearance to let your negative feelings go. Practice different techniques to find out which one works well with you.

Some of the grounding techniques you can try include:

Physical Techniques

- Put your hands in the water, feeling its temperature from your fingertips to the backs of your hands. Try using warm water first, then cold water next. The alternating temperature helps you stay grounded.

- Hold an ice cube in your hands and feel the sensation as it starts melting. An ice cube is an excellent tool to use for grounding techniques with its coldness. It is particularly helpful when dealing with intense feelings.

- Touch or pick up items near you whenever you feel distressed or disassociated. Concentrate on whether it is light or heavy, soft or hard, or warm or cool to the touch. Guessing their colors based on the texture is also an excellent exercise.

- Take a short walk, focusing on your steps. You can concentrate on the feeling as you walk on the ground or silently count your steps. You may also take notice of your footsteps' rhythm each time you put down and lift your foot again.

- Deep breathing is also a grounding technique that helps you keep calm. Take a deep breath, slowly inhaling and exhaling while simultaneously thinking 'in' and 'out.' Feel your lungs getting filled with breath and the air getting pushed back out.

- Perform some exercises or stretches such as jumping up and down, jogging, or other similar activities that move different muscle groups. Notice how each movement makes you feel, keeping your focus on it.

- Savoring each bite of food or drink with you enjoying how they taste and smell. Let the flavors linger on your tongue. Concentrate on them to keep your thoughts away from your intense emotions.

- Take a seat or keep standing. Either way, you can stay now whenever you experience traumatic episodes by focusing on the awareness your body feels. Notice each sensation from head to toe. From the coldness of the glass you hold in your hand to the straight posture you keep your back.

- Listen to your surroundings. The barking of the dogs, the chirping of the birds, each grunt of a machine working, or the gentle thud of footsteps around you. Focus on the conversations you hear, the sounds of the rain pit patting on the roof. All of these helps you stay in the moment and not get lost in your painful memories.

Mental Techniques

- Consider one or two categories, such as mammals, places, girl's names, etc., and mentally list them. List as many items, or things you can think about that belongs to every category you included in the mental exercise.

- Try playing a memory game by looking at a detailed picture such as a cityscape for a few seconds. Take in all details of the photo, then put it face down while you recreate it in your mind. Recreate it as much as possible, or you can list in your mind all the things you can remember.

- Recite a song, poem, quotes, book passages, or anecdotes, anything you can remember. Do this in your head while visualizing each word or silently mouthing it to yourself while shaping every word in your mouth?

- You can exercise mentally with numbers, such as by reciting the multiplication table. You can also count from 1 to 100 or backward. Simple addition or subtraction problems are great as well.

Self-Soothing Skills

Learning some self-soothing skills can also help you stay calm and relaxed when reeling from the memory of narcissistic abuse. By soothing, it means regulating your consuming feelings, so you are back to yourself again. The idea is the same when your parents pat your back while you cry.

Only this time, you do it to yourself. There is a bit of a disadvantage with self-soothing, as you might use addictive behavior as a quick fix. It makes it crucial that you choose healthy things to help you cope with your trauma as self-soothing skills.

Use Positive Associations

The use of positive associations created while performing said grounding exercises could also help you with traumatic episodes. Use cue objects, words, or scents that you have associated with good or safe memories. When you see them or hold them while having an attack, they will remind you that you're safe.

Opposite positive associations, you can use distancing techniques when the cues you made began to have negative associations. These techniques will guide your cues back to safe visualizations. Both techniques may be enhanced when performed with meditation.

Deep Breathing

Breathing exercises have been known to be helpful when you need to calm down. When your emotions are overwhelming, focus on your breath so you can induce relaxation and centering. When you take a deep breath and release it, think of your stressors getting released with every exhalation.

While doing breathing exercises, you may indulge in some meditation or listen to soothing music as a background—both help keep you calm. Thanks to the music, you can stop distracting thoughts from entering your mind.

Containment Exercises

Whenever you feel pain because of intense emotions, you can use containment exercises to separate yourself from these feelings until you are ready to deal with them. With these exercises, you can regain your emotions as they allow you to choose when and where to process them freely.

Containment exercises are a lot like mental exercises. Visualize in your mind an actual container—strong and large—enough to safely hold all your traumatic experiences and painful memories. The container is tightly sealed, which can only be opened when you think it is safe.

The container serves as your locker where you can keep negative emotions throughout the day. You put them inside the box and wait until you dare to examine and process your hidden emotions. With this exercise, you can avoid becoming overwhelmed by anxiety, fear, and dissociation.

Chapter 12:

Effects of Gaslighting

G aslighting is a crazy-making effect that can lead to exploitation, which is sometimes hard to see. The intention of the person using gaslighting is to, in a subtle and organized way, crumble the self-confidence of the victim so that they are not able to act independently. In the end, the victim becomes a robot who only obeys the order of the manipulator.

The emotional damage caused by gaslighting can be enormous on the victim. When a person is exposed to gaslighting for too long, they lose their sense of self-identity, and they start to distrust their judgment and second-guess themselves.

Gaslighting may lead a victim to develop emotional and mental concerns. Self-doubting and confusion can add to anxiety, and this anxiety can lead to depression, post-traumatic stress, and codependency.

The effects of gaslighting can be detrimental to the victim; these effects don't come all at once; they come in three stages: disbelief, defense, and depression. Before we go into these stages, let's take a look at the harmful effects gaslighting has on victims;

Confusion

Gaslighting works when the victim is unaware of it, and the constant use of gaslighting tactics by the narcissist makes the victim gradually bend to their will. Over time, doubts creep into the victims' minds, and with more gaslighting going on, the victim is confused. Though they know something is going wrong, they can't pinpoint exactly what it is.

It is a never-ending cycle for the victims as long as they are in close relation with the narcissist. Confusion results from the narcissist's exploitation of the victim's vulnerabilities. Narcissists keep their victims always second-guessing what they throw at them as they are always alternating between acts of cruelty and acts of kindness.

The narcissists break down victims piece by piece to become more and more unstable, and eventually, victims come to rely on them for comfort and guidance as confusion takes its toll on victims mentally and physically.

Confusion in the victims eventually leads to isolation, as the victims are too confused as to how the whole situation came to be in the first place.

Loss of Confidence

When a person falls victim to a gaslighting narcissist, their confidence starts to erode, and as they may find themselves second-guessing things, the victim develops a heightened sense of self-doubt. Every decision will now be backed with an internal question, "What if I...?"

The victims start to live in fear of doing the wrong things as they are now sensitive to the constant projection, blame, lies, and humiliation of the narcissist. As a result of looking up to the narcissist for approval before taking action, they ask themselves, "Am I too sensitive....?' And because they act with fear, they often end up making mistakes in their activities.

As time progresses, the victim will start showing signs of low confidence; they would find it hard to offer a simple thank you when they are complimented. This happens because of the unconscious emotional damage caused by gaslighting: a victim will reject a positive view of themselves because they have unconsciously accepted the fact that they are unworthy from the narcissist.

A victim will find it hard to hold eye contact with others because they are afraid others will see right through them and notice their flaws. The narcissists have successfully projected a part of themselves onto the victim.

Loss of confidence also makes victims always apologize as they are never doing anything right in the eyes of the narcissist, and to prevent further name-calling and humiliation, they apologize even for the words they say.

Indecision

A typical result of gaslighting is questioning everything, as the victim doesn't know what's real and imagined. This, in turn, means the victim finds it challenging to make the most straightforward choices because they now find it impossible to know what is "right" from what is "wrong."

Victims of gaslighting not only have trouble making big decisions, but simple choices such as brushing their teeth are now also hard to make, as they have been caught up in the narcissist's web of illusion, and they are bonded to the narcissist.

This kind of bond to the narcissist is formed out of the fear that the victim will lose their sense of self. One part of the victim will try to align itself to the needs and choices of the narcissist, while another will try to align itself with the victim's preferences.

Moreover, the narcissist projects their fear of taking responsibility and the need for perfection onto the victim, so the fear of taking responsibility makes it hard to make decisions.

Gradually, victims begin to lose their power to make decisions until they cannot decide anything for themselves. Now they have to rely on the narcissist for guidance and ask the narcissist for permission to do things.

Distrust

As a result of the same victims of gaslighting feel, they try to cover up the fact that mental manipulation is going on in their lives, and when their family and best friends start to notice the changes in them, they deny the subject and cover-up, or they may avoid the issue.

Gaslighting victims start to withhold information from people who mean well because they fear what will happen if they were ever found out by the narcissist. They begin to withdraw from society, and they start to distrust other people.

The victims of gaslighting not only have trouble trusting family and friends, but they also increasingly feel they can't trust themselves either.

Distrust causes victims not only an inability to form new friendships and relationships but also to withdraw themselves into isolation from friends and family.

This particular effect of gaslighting continues to occur even after the victim has successfully eliminated the narcissist from their lives, as when they make new friends, they find it difficult to trust and will always be hypervigilant about relationships.

Melancholy

Gaslighting practiced on the victim over time will take away the happiness and joy of the victims. Narcissists leave their victims afraid, confused, lonely, and unhappy through mental manipulation and emotional abuse.

The victims have the feeling that they used to be a different person, one who was confident and carefree. What the victims don't realize is that anyone who lives under the constant oppression of the gaslighting narcissist can have character change.

This vile act compounds over time to cause a significant personality change in the victims: victims who used to be calm, fun-loving, and the best of themselves are now depressed due to the mental abuse.

Gaslighting causes depression in victims after a while, as the constant letting down, blame-shifting, dissonance, and mental manipulation take their toll on them.

The effects of gaslighting don't come all at once in victims; these effects occur in stages, and victims will go through three steps when they suffer in the hands of a gaslighting narcissist: disbelief, defense, and depression. When depression sets it, the victim discards their own reality, and the narcissist wins.

Stage One: Disbelief

Disbelief is the first reaction of the victim towards gaslighting behavior. They can't figure out what is happening and why the narcissist suddenly changes their attitude towards them. Of course, the narcissists want this because, along the way, they know the victim will submit to their wishes, and they will control the victim's reality.

At first, the narcissist presents a different version of themselves to the victim. In the eyes of the victim, a narcissist is a person full of love, and they will find it hard to believe that a person that has once shown love to them is now something else.

This first stage is a state of total unawareness on the part of the victim. The victim is not aware of the gaslighting that is employed by the narcissist. All that they see is that the narcissist who once supported them and shown love to them is now very critical of them, and any attempt to talk about the reason for the change of attitude is blocked or diverted into something not relevant to the reason why their attitude changed or in worse cases the attempt to talk is met with silence.

At this stage, love-bombing stops, and nitpicking starts: the victims are shocked about the narcissist's radical change of behavior. One minute, the narcissist was the perfect person, and now the narcissist is a shadow of their former selves.

The victim will still try to make sense of everything at this stage and might attribute the sudden change of behavior to another event in the life of the narcissist.

Stage Two: Defense

At this stage, the victim still has a grip on the part of themselves to fight and defend themselves against the gaslighting manipulation.

The narcissist at this point is gaslighting with covert threats, triangulation, and name-calling.

The narcissist is trying hard to make the victim think they are insane at this point, but a part of the victim is working hard to believe this while another part has accepted the fact that the victim is crazy.

This is the stage where gaslighting tactics begin to work, but the victim still has control over a little part of their mind. At this stage, gaslighting has worn out a part of the victim's mind; the victim begins to mentally weaken and starts to give in.

In any case, the narcissist's gaslighting starts to do what it is expected to do, that is, to startle the victim by creating self-doubt and guilt in them. This emotional harm causes the victim, after some time, to lose their sense of the real world and their sense of self. They become lost and incapable of trusting in their own memory. The victim may start to feel shame, and after a while, the victim will feel they are in great danger.

Psychologists believe that nature has built-in coping mechanisms from birth for when we feel we are about to be destroyed.

One of these coping mechanisms is explained as "Stockholm Syndrome," where the victim adapts to the traumatic situation by unconsciously reverting to childhood patterns of behavior and bonds with their abuser as they did with their mother in their childhood when they feel threatened.

Another coping mechanism is "Cognitive Dissonance," where the victim seeks to rationalize the narcissist's behavior.

To defend themselves, victims do two things to cope with the gaslighting:

They rationalize the behavior of the abusive narcissist, and as such, they fall into a state of cognitive dissonance. This is a state of discomfort that occurs when a person holds contradictory ideas or beliefs in their minds at the same time.

Stage Three: Depression

At this stage, gaslighting has taken its full effect, and the victim has now become a shadow of their former selves. They begin to think they can't make decisions anymore; they can't deal with reality any longer, and they withdraw into depression.

By this stage, the victim can barely recognize themselves, and they are rapidly turning into a shadow of their former selves, living inside a war region where they are controlled physically and battered emotionally. The victim starts to avoid people, places, or thoughts and develops a lack of interest in activities that give them happiness and joy. They also begin to relive past experiences.

Chapter 13:

Narcissist Abuse

We are going to explain how narcissistic personality disorder comes to be. This will give you some insight as to how your abuser may have gotten to where they are today. That being said, it is important to understand that most people with a narcissistic personality disorder do not believe they have anything wrong with them. Therefore they very seldom seek treatment. If they do, it will likely not be because you pressured them into it. It is suggested that you use this as an opportunity to understand, rather than as a tool to attempt to show your abuser that they are abusive and to pressure them into seeking treatment.

Causes of Narcissism

Typically, personality disorders are caused by a complex series of issues that lead to the disorder developing. It is hard to predict or determine whether a child will become a narcissist, though there are some things that are believed to contribute to the development of the disorder. Here are the three theories of what goes into the creation of a narcissist.

Theory One: Environment

The first theory involved is their environment. Psychologists and psychotherapists believe that a child's environment can contribute to the potential development of personality disorders, including narcissistic personality disorder. The primary area in the child's environment where these disorders tend to develop is directly in the parent-child relationship. Typically, excessive admiration or excessive criticism toward the child can promote the development of narcissism. If a child is raised by a parent who is a narcissist, they may also learn the behavior and begin to express themselves with narcissistic behavioral patterns. In this case, the person may be on the narcissist spectrum but may not have a full-blown narcissistic personality disorder.

Theory Two: Genetics

As with the majority of illnesses, personality disorders can be inherited by family members. If an individual has one or more people with narcissistic personality disorder in their family, they may be at a higher risk of becoming a narcissist later in their own life. Although this may be an inherited characteristic, there is no way of testing genetics to determine whether or not a person will become or is at risk of becoming a narcissist in their lifetime.

Theory Three: Neurobiology

Neurobiology refers to the connection between the brain, behavior, and thinking. Psychologists, neurologists, and other researchers believe that an individual's neurobiology may encourage them to develop narcissistic personality disorder at some point in their life. Again, there is no way to test a child's brain to determine whether or not they are at risk of developing narcissistic personality disorder in their lifetime. Some theories believe that traumatic life events early in life can change the individuals' neurobiology, thus making them more likely to become a narcissist later in life. This can happen as a result of the trauma itself or because of the way their parents may change their behavior toward the child. For example, if the parents' divorce is traumatic to the child and the child becomes neglected by one or both parents, this can contribute to narcissism. Alternatively, if the child experienced a loss or a personal trauma, such as a serious illness or injury, and one or both parents coddled the child long after the injury attempting to protect them from further dangers, this could also contribute to the potential onset of narcissism later in life.

Risk Factors

Many will not receive a diagnosis because they genuinely believe that there is nothing wrong with them and it is everyone else who has a problem. Despite this being the prime age for diagnosis, some children may begin to show narcissistic traits as they are growing up. Some of these may be typical to their age and will never go on to develop narcissistic personality disorder, whereas other children will.

Anyone can be a narcissist, no matter what their age, gender, religion, or ethnic background may be. The disorder is not related to the demographics of the individual so much as one or a combination of the causes listed above.

The general consensus agreed upon by doctors and psychologists is that the biggest risk factor leading to the potential development of narcissism later in life is parenting. Parents who are neglectful, overindulgent, abusive, or pathological have a tendency to treat their children in a way that results in the child never actually overcoming the grand sense of self that all children have. In general, children are expected to be more self-indulgent because this is how they learn about their own identity and how they fit into the world. As they grow older, this sense of self-indulgence should fade away over time as they find their answers and begin fitting in. For those who have not been raised in a household where they had access to healthy parenting, either as a result of excessive or neglectful parenting or as a result of constant traumatic abuse, are at risk of not growing past this self-indulgent behavior. Instead, they use it as a way to feel good in spite of their parents' leading them to believe that they are unworthy of love, or as a way to continue feeling good as a result of their parents leading them to believe that they are special over everyone else and deserve to be treated as such.

Complications

There are many complications that an individual will face if they are diagnosed with narcissistic personality disorder. Of these complications, the majority of them are rooted in social behavior. Individuals with narcissistic personality disorder struggle to maintain relationships, have difficulty at work or school, and may resort to drug or alcohol misuse. The narcissistic personality goes untreated, and in many cases, even when it is addressed. This is because, in most cases, narcissists are incapable of admitting and accepting that they are narcissistic. Doing so would result in their entire reality crashing in around them. Furthermore, transitioning from a self-serving lifestyle that others feed into as a result of their abuse and into one that requires them to think of anyone other than themselves is virtually impossible. The amount of pain and loss they would feel from this transition would be more than they are willing to endure. The only time a narcissist may actually seek support is if they have literally lost everyone in their life and are no longer able to reel people into their abuse cycle. In this case, they may be willing to consider therapy. At that rate, therapy is not guaranteed to be effective as they may just use this as a bargaining chip to confirm that they are "doing better" when, in fact, they are not.

Another major complication that narcissists face lies in shame. As a result of their upbringing and how they were taught, every single narcissist faces shame in their childhood. Where this shame comes from depends on what caused their narcissism in the first place, but it virtually always results in them feeling the need to "delete" their true self in favor of a false persona. This behavior essentially supports the narcissist in splitting away from the aspects of themselves that they are ashamed of and supports them in creating a mask that they feel should fix what has caused the shame in the first place.

If the narcissist was raised in a neglectful household, the shame would lie within virtually every aspect of the narcissist. As a result, the repeating feeling of shame and neglect would create a sense of trauma in the child that would cause them to want to discard any aspect of themselves that brought them shame or, in their opinion, resulted in them being neglected. Their true self: the parts that they were ashamed of and that they feel lead to the neglect, would then be denied in favor of a false self or mask that would ultimately redesign their profile and make them seem likable to everyone.

If the narcissist was raised in an overly coddled household, the shame would lie within any aspect of the child that was not coddled by the parents. So, if they were deemed an academic genius, anything they struggled with that made them feel as though they were incompetent or uneducated would cause shame. They would become addicted to the praise and the attention they received when they were behaving according to their parents' standards and would feel ashamed about any aspect of themselves that did not live up to what their parents felt was acceptable. This would either be aspects of themselves that contradicted what the parents were proud of, or any aspect of themselves that were ignored or even punished out of them by the parents. The true self, then, would include all of those aspects, whereas the false self would seek to discard them in favor of being entirely likable and admirable to their parents.

If the child was abused growing up, any number of aspects of themselves could bring them shame. This can be even further amplified and reinforced if the abuse experienced by the child was also narcissistic abuse. In general, these aspects will directly relate to what they felt caused the abuse. This could lead to a wide range of aspects of themselves that they would then want to discard or decimate in favor of becoming a different variation of themselves that would be void of all of the aspects that they felt lead to their abuse in the first place.

Many complications can arise in the face of the shame that narcissists feel. Because they blame this part of themselves for the pain and trauma they experienced at various points in their childhood, they feel strongly about the need to hide the true self in favor of the false self, which they feel will earn them greater respect and better treatment from everyone else. Because they embody this false self entirely, this leads to their sense of believing that they are special: because in their eyes, unlike everyone else, they have worked so hard to discard the "bad" parts of who they were.

Prevention and Treatment

Preventing and treating narcissistic personality disorder is challenging since the majority of these individuals will never become properly diagnosed. If the disorder is related to parenting styles, the parent may be unwilling to admit to there being a problem as well, creating further difficulties for the child to get the required care. Still, some preventative measures and treatments are available for narcissistic personality disorder.

Chapter 14:

Coping with Narcissist Abuse

I f you have ever been in a relationship with, or are experiencing narcissistic abuse, then you probably know how hard it is to leave. You know what you need to do, you think about how you can escape, and you gain the courage to do it, but then, you don't. You don't because something holds you back in. You sit there and think of all the good memories, then think about what would happen after you actually left, then you think about all the things that haven't happened yet, and wonder if things will change if you stayed due to whatever excuse you come up with. This is another form of fear. Your mind has you trapped as a result of the abuse to the point where, when you do decide to or try to leave, you feel a flood of panic. The fear is something many of us can't seem to overcome, so we stay in the relationship hoping that things will get better or that things will be okay. But it never does, so you start from the beginning, getting ready to leave again. It's a vicious cycle that no one should have to go through. If you find yourself sitting there most of the time asking yourself, "should I stay, should I go," then you most likely already know the answer to this and should go. Things don't get better; they only repeat themselves. The narcissist you are involved with will always make promises they can't keep, and they will always build you up for the main purpose of thrashing you down.

Devastation is difficult to manage, but with the right support, you will get through all the stages and reach a point where you view your ex as a person you knew but has no hold over you. I promise you that if you reclaim your power after getting through the dark side of your breakup, you will come to a realization that without sacrifices, you will stay stuck. No one likes to be stuck, and no one needs to feel the way you do right now. So, get up, release yourself, and become one with who you are by starting the first stage of the breakup.

Devastation

So, we have already talked about devastation, but did we talk about ways to get through it the easiest way possible? No. When we are devastated, we don't want to do anything, eat anything, speak to anyone, and we would rather drown our sorrows under cozy blankets and cry into our pillows. Devastation comes in a few different stages and can come all at once or one by one. First (or last) comes the shock that you are actually done, that your relationship is actually over. Memories will pool inside your mind and flush you back to what was. Next, you may feel numb or cry (a lot), with the feeling of not caring about anything. Your eyes may hurt, you may not be able to sleep, which makes you unable to concentrate on anything, and you could withdraw from the rest of the world because you would rather do this alone than have anyone see you as pathetic as you feel. Next, anger sets in. You may become bitter to people around you and forget to take care of your needs, like clean the house or get dressed. Anger will consume you if you let it, but this is part of the process of healing. To get past this feeling, you feel like a "rebound" will help you get out of this slump. So, you put on a fake smile, get dressed up, and go out on the town to get under someone else, so that you feel the affection you crave so much. This is called denial. You are in denial about your feelings. You think you are ready, but you are not. If you do this, you will most likely end up with the same type of person you were just with, thus resulting in more damage to yourself later down the road.

As much as devastation hurts, and you may want to do everything to stop feeling that aching pain in your chest. The best way to get through this stage is to learn techniques that will help you deal with these overwhelming emotions. It is important to remember that although this stage is needed for a successful final stage if you let yourself feel this way for too long, you will never recover. So, instead of remembering your lowest point, reminiscing about the good and bad memories, remembering all your fights and all your efforts, or trying to come with answers to why you were so badly treated, stop. If you continue to do this, the pain only escalates and keeps you in the devastation stage longer than you need to be there.

Instead, try these tactics to help you speed up the process of devastation:

1. Closure

This stage of devastation may be so hard for some people that they often go back to their spouse during this stage. After all the crying and the anger, maybe a couple of rebounds, they decide to go back. This is not healthy because the next time you leave, you will have to start this process all over again, and I don't need to remind you what happens to our brains when we are under this type of stress. So, just end it. If you have made the decision to leave, then do that. Get your closure, write letters (send them or don't), say your goodbyes (physically or to yourself), and do whatever you need to gain some sort of closure. But don't go back.

2. Externalize

It revolves around knowing and understanding how you feel and being patient with these feelings. It's about accepting the hurt that you feel but not clinging to it. Knowing that there will be better days, and right now, it is okay to let it all out.

3. Appropriate process

This is a necessary process to help you cope with the devastation because it allows you to make sure you are not obsessing over the breakup and your feelings. It comes in five steps:

➢ Admit the pain or anger
➢ Vent, and let it out to the people who are most supportive - or write about it.
➢ Determine your response to your emotions (are you going to sit here and feel sorry for yourself, or are you going to try to get up and take care of yourself today?)
➢ Stick to your goals, and your plan to recovering and making it through this first stage of devastation
➢ Forget it. Shift your thoughts to something else, something more positive. You can only learn to forget once the other steps are taken care of.

4. Distraction

Devastation will destroy your sense of accomplishment and hold you from doing things you used to enjoy. This stage in the process is to fight back - do the opposite of what you feel. So, if you feel like sitting in bed all day, get up and sit on the couch or go outside for the day. Distract your mind with telephone calls to loved ones, play crosswords, exercise, write, draw, etc. Do something creative, and don't allow yourself to sit with this pain.

5. Maintain your schedule

Whatever your routine was before, continue with it. If it is hard to fully maintain a routine right now, just do a couple a day, then gradually increase your strength to move on to the next thing you used to do. For example, if you used to wake up and go for a run, come home, shower, get ready for work, go to work, come home and make dinner, then read a book. Start by just getting up and going for a light walk and having a brisk shower. Day by day, increase your routine to one more thing on that list.

6. Find a place that doesn't trigger you.

If your breakup consisted of them moving, and you are stuck with all the memories no matter where you look, consider moving or staying with a friend for a while. If you had to move, and it hurts to go out and see the places you guys walked or went on dates, avoid these places and find somewhere new to go. Just don't avoid it forever.

7. Give in to the need for closeness without sexual contact.

The fastest way to get through this stage is physical closeness. So, if you have a child, cuddle them; if you have a best friend, ask for lots of hugs. When you need a shoulder to cry on, reach out to someone you trust. Along with this physical closeness, bonding with people you trust is a bonus in this recovery.

8. Avoid all things sexual

Although physical closeness is essential for recovering from a narcissist breakup, sexual entanglement with someone can make things worse. If you haven't completely moved on, you may feel shame, guilt, and even more anger. We want to avoid this as much as possible.

Devastation is the first stage of recovery, and it may also be the hardest. However, when you make it through this stage, you can move on to start taking better care of yourself, which will make you feel good. In short, you must let your feelings sink in, don't fight them, take care of your well-being, and stay off the internet or forums (at least for now). The last thing you want to do is overwhelm yourself with research that reminds you of your narcissistic relationship.

Allow Yourself to Grieve

Believe it or not, crying and tears are beneficial to your recovery. Crying is scientifically proven to rid your body of stress. When you let your other emotions in, this also helps with the grieving process. However, if you hold your emotions in, you are making connections in your brain that suggest holding it in is a better solution and will actually cause more problems for you later. When people hold their tears and anger in, they never learn to release or let go. Instead, they teach themselves that it is okay to hold it in, which can result in an outburst later. Have you ever cried so hard, then after you get this foggy feeling, but it feels as though a weight has almost lifted? This is because you have relieved yourself of the tension or stress that you feel.

Chapter 15:

Complex Post-Trauma Stress Symptoms

P ost-traumatic stress disorder is a result of some type of traumatic event. You've probably heard about it associated with war veterans, but it can also be caused by physical assaults, rape, car accidents, or emotional abuse. Really, any kind of disturbing or upsetting event that occurs can result in PTSD, particularly if it overwhelms your ability to cope with what happened. What's more, women are twice as likely to suffer from PTSD, and they also experience a longer duration of symptoms and more sensitivity to any triggers that remind them of the event. PTSD, as you've probably commonly heard of it, happens after a single traumatic incident, but there is another form, called Complex PTSD or C-PTSD, that results from repeated trauma over months or years. This is the type of PTSD we'll be talking about, though both types of PTSD share similar symptoms and treatments.

The effects of C-PTSD can be drastic if left untreated, and aside from the mental health implications of the condition, it can also lead to physical health problems. You might suffer from headaches, stomach problems, and sexual dysfunction, among other things. What happens with C-PTSD is that you do not only remember what happened; it's as if you're back in the incident you endured. It's like you went back in time and are living through that moment again. Your body responds as if you are too, and in response to it, the body produces the stress hormones that result in a whole range of physical, mental, and emotional symptoms.

C-PTSD in Women

Women who are suffering from the effects of C-PTSD often don't seek help, sometimes for years, and then, when they do, the condition is frequently misdiagnosed or missed altogether by the health professional. It is also not uncommon that the woman herself may not be aware of the problem.

Women tend to internalize their problems, and rather than look outward to their situation, they might just decide that what they're suffering from is just a product of their own personality, thoughts, and emotions. They don't realize that there is a concrete problem from which they're suffering. For that reason, it's important to understand the causes, symptoms, and treatments for this condition. It's hard, though, because there is still a stigma against most mental health disorders, and that's particularly true for women who suffer from PTSD following an assault or C-PTSD following years of emotional abuse. Moreover, women are frequently traumatized further by the professionals in whom they confide. They might be questioned about the veracity of what they're saying and their reaction to the situation.

Differences in PTSD and C-PTSD Between Men and Women

As with many diseases and conditions, there is a difference in how women experience C-PTSD compared to men. Women, for example, are more likely to experience depression and anxiety while also having more difficulty feeling and dealing with their emotions.

Additionally, they often avoid activities and things that remind them of what happened to them. Alternatively, men are more likely to turn to alcohol or drugs to mask their emotional response to trauma.

The key to treating C-PTSD is to be educated about how it can affect you. It is a treatable condition, but you first have to recognize that you have a problem. This can be difficult for women since they frequently feel a need to be perfect and are often reluctant to admit they have something that they perceive as a weakness. It's not just their perception either; women are constantly told they need to do it all and must do it well. That's an unrealistic expectation and can create rather intense pressure. Before we talk about some of the treatment options for C-PTSD, let's look at some of the more common symptoms for women and men.

C-PTSD Symptoms

For C-PTSD to be diagnosed, a patient must experience symptoms for at least a month, though they could be suffering for months or years before going for a diagnosis. Symptoms might not appear immediately, either. When they do, they can typically be categorized into three types:

1. Re-experiencing the trauma, which typically occurs in the form of intrusive and distressing recollections of a single event or multiple events. These recollections could come in nightmares or through flashbacks.

2. Emotional numbness and avoidance of places, people, or activities that remind the individual of what happened to them.

3. Increased arousal, which can result in difficulty concentrating or sleeping, as well as feeling jumpy and being easily irritated and angered.

Typically, the traumatic events that cause PTSD, in general, include exposure to actual or threatened death, serious injury, or sexual violation, but trauma also occurs with long-term emotional abuse, where the individual's fight or flight response was repeatedly stimulated, eventually resulting in complex-PTSD. In this situation, the brain doesn't distinguish between physical trauma and emotional trauma; it only reads your fear and responds accordingly. It also tends to read anxiety as fear and responds with a cascade of physiological responses, including the production of stress hormones. The chronic production of stress hormones has dramatic physical and emotional effects. It's also important to note that the threat or abuse doesn't have to be directed at the individual involved, and both kinds of PTSD can also result when someone witnesses a traumatic event or emotional abuse. The specific symptoms for a diagnosis in each of these general categories include the following:

Re-Experiencing the Trauma

Re-experiencing trauma can take the following forms:

- Spontaneous, recurrent, and involuntary memories of the traumatic event that intrude into an individual's consciousness. For example, experiencing a memory can happen when a trigger is perceived. In children, this might be seen in how they play. Their play may take the form of themes or aspects of the trauma they suffered.

- Recurrent and distressing dreams related to the traumatic event- This might mean dreaming specifically about the event, but it can also just be dreams that have a feeling similar to it. In children, this may take the form of dreams that don't have any recognizable content.

- Dissociative reactions—such as flashbacks—where the individual experiences the memory as if it were actually happening again- This typically causes the individual to become fully immersed in the flashback.

- Intense, prolonged psychological distress from being exposed to either internal or external triggers that symbolize the traumatic events.

- Specific physiological reactions to reminders of the trauma they suffered. For example, some individuals might become nauseated when stimulated by a reminder of what they suffered.

Avoidance of Distressing Memories

This is a more typical response for women and can be diagnosed based on the presence of two or more of the following symptoms:

- An incapability to recall certain significant aspects of the traumatic event that cannot be accounted for by a head injury, alcohol, or drugs.

- Persistent and often exaggerated negative beliefs or expectations about oneself, other people, or the world in general. For example, the person might say, "I am bad," "No one can be trusted," or "The world is a dangerous place."

- Persistent feelings of self-blame or blaming others regarding what caused the consequences of the traumatic events

- Persistent feelings of fear, horror, anger, shame, or guilt

- Diminished interest in participating in significant activities

- Feeling detached or estranged from other people.

- A persistent inability to experience positive emotions

Changes in Arousal and Reactivity

This can occur in both men and women and can be diagnosed based on two or more of the following changes:

- Irritability and a marked increase in aggression

- Reckless or self-destructive behavior.

- Hypervigilance.

- An exaggerated startle response.

- Problems concentrating.

- Significant distress or impairment in social or occupational areas of functioning that cannot be attributed to the effects of medication, drugs, alcohol, or some kind of medical condition like a traumatic brain injury

Treatment Options for PTSD and C-PTSD

There are several treatment options available for both kinds of PTSD that have been shown to be effective for helping women cope with their symptoms. These include both psychological and medication-based treatments. The first step in treating PTSD (either kind), however, is to diagnose the condition. To diagnose PTSD, your doctor will begin with a physical examination to check for any medical problems that might be related to your symptoms; this is to rule out the possibility that your symptoms are caused by other conditions and not PTSD. Once those physical ailments are ruled out, the doctor may refer you to a psychologist for an evaluation. That will involve talking about your symptoms and the events that likely produced them. Finally, the psychologist will make use of the diagnostic criteria listed in the Diagnostic and Statistical Manual of Mental Disorders (DSM-5).

A diagnosis requires that you were exposed to trauma either directly, as a witness, or through learning someone close to you was traumatized. Additionally, you might have been repeatedly exposed to graphic details of a traumatic event, as might be the case with first responders. Along with exposure to the trauma of some kind, your symptoms must have been persistent for more than one month, and they must create significant problems in your ability to function in the different areas of your life.

Normalizing involves the following:

- Recognizing and accepting that physical pain may be a symptom. People with either kind of PTSD can struggle with migraines, back pain, or stomach and digestive issues.

- Recognizing and accepting that flashbacks or nightmares might occur and that they can be triggered by sounds, smells, or even a phrase that someone else says.

- By normalizing the symptoms, it can help alleviate the patient's sense of guilt. The treatment is still a long process, but it begins with hope. The goals of the treatment program include helping you regain a sense of control over your life by utilizing the following strategies:

- Teaching skills to address the symptoms as they occur.

- Helping you think more positively about yourself, other people, and the world in general.

- Learning better coping strategies for symptoms.

- Treating other symptoms related to the traumatic experience, like depression, anxiety, or substance abuse.

Chapter 16:
Letting Go and Moving On

Whether or not you feel like you have been the victim of narcissistic abuse, being in a relationship with a narcissist is not without its challenges and may lead to an unhappy end, or rather, it could lead to you staying in it, even when it contradicts who you are as a person and your dreams and goals of successful relationships and a happy life. Whatever you are feeling at this moment as you read this book, letting go of your relationship may not feel like your first choice, and that's okay.

For some readers, there is no question that it is time to pack up and go. It all depends on a person's wants and needs and their ability to be honest with the truth of what is really going on in their marriage or partnership. It can take some time to understand the dynamics of your narcissistic partnership after you have identified that you are in one.

Moving forward can be a challenge, and many people will struggle with putting an end to this type of relationship, mainly due to the reality of narcissistic abuse and emotional manipulation. It really is about who you are, what your experience is, and what is going on right now to help you understand the best choice forward for you.

The following will help you identify when it might be good to leave a narcissistic relationship and how to put an end to it so that you don't keep coming back to it and repeating the same patterns repeatedly. A lot of that experience requires getting help and support and eventually a period of recovery from the narcissistic relationship so that you don't end up with the same type of person again, repeating the patterns in an entirely new relationship.

When and How to End the Relationship

The time is right for you to leave if you have undergone any emotional, mental or physical abuse, if you have identified serious cycles of manipulation or narcissistic issues that never change, if you are sacrificing your own personal power, integrity, success, and desires, or if you feel like you are being taken advantage of on a regular basis to support someone else's fantasies of who they are. There are a lot of ways that narcissism from within your relationship can affect your quality of life, your personal views, your self-worth, and more, and it is not worth it to stick around hoping that your partner will change and be more what you need. They don't care about what you need. They will only ever care about what they need.

If you have tried for a long time to help your partner identify their issue and help them "heal" their problem to no avail, then it is time to let go and move on. It is important to recognize that you can never heal someone for them; they have to do the work to heal themselves. Being a supportive partner is always a good thing, but if you are familiar with how your patterns of support have enabled your narcissistic partner to stay in their preferred role and behavior patterns, then you need to admit that you are at the end of the rope so that you can heal on your own terms and find a happier lifestyle.

The stages of detaching from your partner can go on for a while as you begin to identify the issues and start to pull away, changing your role in the situation and recognizing your readiness to end things. It can be uncomfortable for your partner, who will make it uncomfortable for you as a result, and so understanding some of the stages that you will likely go through will help you prepare for moving on.

Detachment from a Narcissist: Stages

First Stage:

When the rose-colored glasses come off, and you stop accepting blame, guilt, or shame in your relationship, you begin to resurface and "wake up" to what has really been going on. In the first stage, you are "seeing" more clearly all of the patterns, the covert and subversive ridicule, and all of the tools of manipulation to push you away and punish you, and then pull you back in and adore you. This is the stage of awareness of the problem and the first shift and change in the situation.

Second Stage:

You may still have feelings for your partner at this point, even a seriously deep love bond; however, your usual desire to please them no matter what will begin to be replaced with the feeling of anger and even resentment that they are so consistently and continuously demanding of your admiration, adoration and pleasing them. The love may still be there, but you are not so "naïve" anymore.

Signals of the Second Stage:

- Your partner's lies no longer have an effect on you and feel obvious and pathetic.

- You are no longer succumbing to the manipulation tools.

- You regain a sense of self-worth and feel you deserve to be treated better.

- You begin to fight for yourself more and create more conflict with your partner.

- You begin to regain and rebuild your self-confidence and self-esteem.

Third Stage:

Your confidence is being reborn, and you feel better about yourself and your choices. You may have already joined a support group at this time or started to see a counselor to help with your growth and are feeling more empowered emotionally and mentally. You can better focus on your own wants and needs and start seeing how life would be if you are not involved with your narcissistic partner.

Signals of the third stage:

- You cannot stand to be around your partner.

- You no longer feel an obsessive love or strong love bond.

- If they begin to push your buttons or act inappropriately, you will either have no reaction and not care or retaliate and lash out against them.

- Enjoy more time with friends, in support groups, engage in classes or group meet-ups that support your interests

- You will start to make decisions to support yourself without concerning yourself with your partner's preferences or interests.

- You will begin to make your move to let go and move on by planning your out and getting your ducks in a row.

Fourth Stage:

This is the end of the relationship when your focus becomes facing your future without your partner. At this point, you may have cut the cords, moved out, separated, begun the divorce proceedings, etc. This is the stage when you will have cut them off and out of your life and when you can begin to feel new and like yourself again. You will not want anything to do with your partner, and in some cases, you may have to maintain some kind of contact (if you have children together).

The Overall Process of Letting Go and Moving On:

This process won't occur for anyone overnight. You can end up living in the cycle of one stage for a long time until you are resolved to move forward into the next stage. Being stuck in these processes is highly common, and there is a way to help you ease through a little bit better so that you don't stay stuck for longer than you need to be.

As you begin to consider letting go and moving on, hang onto those thoughts and let yourself feed into them. You are allowed to imagine your life differently, apart from your partner, and it can help you to build steam and momentum if you continually consider the process of cutting cords and stepping forward. It helps to keep fueling your self-esteem and doing things that will help you support yourself in the process. Follow these steps to help:

1. Think about it. Let yourself fuel your exit with self-esteem building and thoughts about moving on. Build momentum so

that you can keep revisiting why you are having these thoughts to begin with.

2. Use a journal or a notebook to write out all of the experiences you want to have, the life you want to live, the places you want to go, and where you want to be successful in your life. Start to write down and consider the kind of partnership and partner you would like to experience. You can even jot down all of the aspects of your current relationship and then make a comparison between what you have and what you really want. Getting into the habit of journaling about you and what you want can help you refocus your life goals and ambitions and further motivate you to let go of the relationship that is hurting your choices and chances for a healthy and successful life.

3. Reflect. Explore your relationship and ask yourself what part, or role, you have played in the experience. The narcissist may be manipulative, toxic, and cunning, but it certainly always takes two to tango, and so it might help you to be honest and identify what ways you have supported the toxicity of your relationship. How have you not lived up to your own standards of love and life? How have you enabled this behavior? What can you do to shift these patterns? Spend time with these thoughts and truly reflect on your own energy in the relationship. Write it down in your journal and begin to create awareness about your role in the partnership. You don't want to fall for the narcissist again, and knowing where you fall for the traps can help you resist them in the future.

4. Find supportive literature. There are countless books out there that aren't just about overcoming a narcissistic relationship, but that are also about empowering yourself, finding the career of your dreams, learning new skills and hobbies, and so on. You can begin to reclaim your identity and your sense of pride and joy in your life by seeking out self-improvement books and literature that will empower you and give you strength.

5. Spend time with others. Connect with your family, friends, co-workers, support groups, etc., and talk about it. Feel free to be yourself around your network of loving and supportive people to help you feel that you are not going to be alone when you walk away and move forward.

Chapter 17:

Maintaining a Healthy Relationship

I f you are already in an unbalanced relationship and want it to change, check out some of these tips.

Take A Good Look At The Relationship

Is it worth pursuing? Is it unbalanced because you no longer love and respect each other? Is it because you've grown apart?

In addition to answering those questions, you have to recognize that certain behaviors like:

- Swearing or yelling at you

- Harassing statements that are directed toward you

- Interrogating or degrading you in any way

- Attacking your self-esteem and that of your loved ones

- Blaming you for the things that go wrong in his or her life (or in general)

- Extreme jealousy

- Gaslighting

- Threatening you in any way (specifically physical or sexual abuse)

- Threats to your family members or friends

- Threats to your kids or pets

- Controlling behavior

- Isolating you from your loved ones

- Controlling you with money or any other means

are not healthy.

Be Clear & Honest With One Another

If you want something to change, you can't lie to the other person or hold in your feelings. You have to offer up your feelings and allow your partner the same respect. Use "I statements": "I feel that..." "This behavior makes me feel that I..."

Not only that, offer up examples of why you feel this way. Don't just give him or her general statements. The more specific, the more of a chance that you'll get a positive change

Consider The Option of "Miscommunication"

Sometimes, things are not how we perceive them to be. If you think that your partner isn't being considerate because he isn't texting you back when you ask questions or because you always have to come up with the plan of action, consider this:

He might just be clueless. I'm not making excuses for your partner. I'm just urging you to be communicative and open-minded. It could just be a horrible, horrible case of miscommunication.

Keep In Mind That We Shouldn't "Change" People

We can't change anyone. They have to be willing to change themselves. You can't force someone to act the way that you want – especially adults. We can change the way we do things, and we can express how we feel and what we need. However, it is up to your partner what he or she wants to do with that information.

Try To Restore Balance To Yourself First

We have to treat ourselves with respect before we expect others to respect us. This is a statement that we often take for granted. We expect others to immediately be respectful toward us, but we don't take care of ourselves.

Reflection is an important step in fixing any relationship. Look within yourself to find what you can do to be happy. Listen to your instincts and trust them. Be open to what your reflection reveals about you and what you need. Find healthy stress relief techniques and treat your body right. These things will lead to a happier life and will lead you to a happy relationship.

Insecurity and Jealousy

Some people may say that the reason for their behavior is insecurity and jealousy. This is not an excuse for treating anyone in a cruel or abusive manner. However, if you deal with insecurity and jealousy at their roots, you can control those behaviors. Counseling will help with these, but there are some things that you can do at home. The first step is to recognize insecurity and jealousy.

Insecurity is a lack of confidence or assurance. You can also call it self-doubt, anxiety, or a lack of confidence. If you are feeling insecure, there is more of a chance that you will develop unhealthy levels of jealousy while you are in a relationship.

There are many different types of people, and we all handle our insecurities in different ways. We can categorize most people into six different categories based on how they handle what they view as their shortcomings:

- People who take those insecurities as a challenge (to better themselves so that they can overcome them),

- People that use humor as a defense mechanism,

- People who just surround themselves with positivity and pretend that they don't have any insecurities at all,

- People who lie about themselves in order to cover up any insecurities (I mean, outlandish wild tales!),

- People who verbally doubt themselves and put themselves down, and

- People who act out because of their insecurities in order to cover them up.

Most of us strive for the first category but end up falling into one of the latter ones. That doesn't mean that we can't change, though.

The Most Important Relationship That You Should Rescue

The most important relationship that should be mended after you leave an abusive relationship is your own relationship with yourself. You need to be able to fix the damage done to your self-esteem because of all of that emotional and mental abuse. Because of that, I want to talk about what you can do to build your confidence:

Self-confidence is a trait that we all take for granted. We rarely think about the ways that self-confidence helps us in our daily lives. One of the most important ways that it helps us is by helping us overcome our fears.

When we improve and build up our self-esteem and confidence level, it can really help us pursue our dreams. We will all fear certain things in our lives. Sometimes it is a phobia buried deep in our subconscious (fear of the unknown, the dark, clowns, being alone, etc.). Other times, we can easily overcome some of our fears by building up our strengths and by being confident in ourselves.

Let's talk about how we can do that. How we can build up that self-assurance so that we can be happy with ourselves is the first step to being happy with your life. Here are some simple steps that you can take to start that process. Mind you, you don't have to do these in any order.

Choose a couple off of the list to try first. If it doesn't work immediately, give them about a week to really have an effect. Keep up with the ones you feel most comfortable with, and drop the ones that aren't working for you. This is your life and your happiness. Do what feels good (and healthy) for you.

1. Become a master at something.

Learning, practicing, and pursuing things that you feel passionate about helps to liberate your mind while focusing it on something specific. This practice will help you focus on other things as well. Practice makes perfect, right?

Studies have shown that it takes approximately 10,000 hours before we can master a specific skill. That is a lot of practicing and a lot of time to focus your mind on a specific task.

If you use this practice time with a task that inspires you, it is time well spent, and you will find it easier to focus. Don't know what activity or skill to choose? Answer some of the questions below to help you zone in on what you feel passionate about:

- Are you a creative person? Do you like to create things with your hands?

- Have you always wanted to try a particular sport or physical activity?

- What hobbies do you enjoy doing when you are by yourself?

- Which of your skills are friends and family members always commenting on?

- Is there something that you enjoy doing, which you would also be inclined to create? For example, are you an avid reader? Would you like to try your hand at writing a book?

2. Play dress-up.

When you feel presentable, and when you dress nicely, you can feel like you're ready to take on the rest of the world. You don't have to go out and buy something expensive or fancy. Casual clothes can be presentable too. You have to find the balance between comfortable and well-dressed.

Creating your own sense of style can help increase your confidence level too. Bring out your personality in your clothes. Don't be afraid to think outside of the box – as long as it goes with the dress code at work. If you're not interested in being fashionable or focusing on your appearance at all, just keep in mind that it's not bad to be known for having a clean and professional appearance.

3. Create an image of how you picture yourself.

When people say that you should "dress for the job that you want, not the job that you have," what they mean is that you should create a self-image of success.

If you can and if you have the software, create an image on your computer. Place yourself in the position that you want to be in five years from now or fifteen years from now. These mental images that we have for success are great ways to motivate ourselves to work harder and work better. Making these mental images into visual and tangible images that you can reference every day will make you feel great.

4. Squash those negative thoughts.

Negativity is your worst enemy. Be aware of how you talk about yourself and how you think of yourself. Negative thoughts can be anything from "I want to quit this" to "I look and feel gross today." The first step to stopping negative thoughts is to recognize this type of self-talk.

The second step is to visualize yourself actively stopping these types of thoughts from entering your mind. You can picture anything that works for you, including (but not limited to):

- Picturing these thoughts as water and stopping them with a dam inside your head,

- Imagining these thoughts as bugs and squashing them with a big boot or a stiletto heel, and

- Visualizing these thoughts as cannonballs and shooting them far away.

Conclusion:

Emotional abuse can be every bit as damaging as physical abuse. In fact, the scars can last longer, and it can take longer to identify since there are many ways for a partner to be emotionally abusive. Often they will dress it up as care and concern, but, in fact, it's all about control. For whatever reason, they feel the need to control your life and destroy your self-esteem and question your own emotional health.

Many emotional abusers have suffered similar treatment at the hands of parents, friends, family, or colleagues, although not all abusers were themselves victims of emotional abuse. Whatever the reason for this behavior, it is not acceptable, and you do not have to tolerate it, although it can be very difficult to escape from, since the abuser may not even realize they have a problem, or if they do, they may be unwilling to change.

It is possible to recover from emotional abuse and be happy again, as long as you can let go of the past and decide on new boundaries and expectations for future relationships. You can be happy again – and indeed, you deserve to be!

As we end this book, I would like to reiterate some points in recovering from Emotional Abuse:

1. The first step is to recognize the problem and then find out as much information about emotional abuse as you can from books and the Internet.

2. Do not hesitate to seek help from a qualified counselor, therapist, or support group, and be prepared to ask a lot of questions.

3. It is imperative that you always tell your friends and family what is going on, even if they are not very sympathetic or understanding. If they do not know, others may expect them to know or be afraid they will become a victim of Emotional Abuse – especially children! The more evidence of the problem there is, the more likely it will be that someone else will take action on your behalf if you are still experiencing it by yourself.

4. Seek professional help if things do not improve, or your abuser becomes more aggressive as time goes on – which is often the case. Most abusive people are totally unaware of the damage they cause. If you tell them you want to make a change, it's not always easy for them (even if they are willing) to change their ways, especially without professional intervention and close supervision.

5. The same applies if you are still experiencing other forms of abuse at the same time as Emotional Abuse – it is not uncommon for perpetrators of all types of abuse to engage in more than one form at once, although there may be some differences in intensity and severity between the different types.

6. If you are still experiencing Emotional Abuse, there is no need to let it continue. Never be afraid to speak the truth about what is happening in your life, and never do anything that you

feel uncomfortable about or make you want to undo an action later on.

7. Do not give up: there's always hope.

Well, you have reached the end of our journey through this book – a journey that has helped hundreds of thousands of people recover from Emotional Abuse and get their lives back on track! I hope it has been helpful, and I wish you the very best in your recovery and future relationships.

Narcissistic Abuse

What the Victims Need to Know to Break the Cycle and Recovery from Emotional and Psychological Abuse

Bianca Sutton

Introduction

N arcissistic abuse is a form of abuse that is difficult to identify and heal from. Narcissists are natural born actors, and they use their special assets to manipulate their victims into believing their behavior is justified. They often come across as charismatic, likable, and charming in public, but there's another side to them that they only show behind closed doors where the true nature of their personality is revealed. According to the Merriam-Webster Dictionary, narcissistic abuse is: "The condition of suffering from chronic or repeated devaluation of self-worth by a primary caretaker, with the resulting in development of narcissistic personality traits."

While in essence this definition may be true, the root cause cannot be attributed to one person and narcissism can develop as a result of different factors that play a role in shaping personality. While some may argue that it is merely a manifestation of a personality disorder, others believe that upbringing and environment contribute to its development. It's not as simple as pointing a finger at one person and blaming him/her for the inevitable misery a victim or two may experience. At times, it's hard to detect, but if you see the signs of narcissism in any relationship, be it intimate or professional, let it be a warning that you might end up with someone who is abusive.

In current society, everyone easily comes across a narcissist. The internet has given us an easy way to seek out potential partners that we might not have otherwise found. Some people fall into bad relationships because they are not aware of the traits of a narcissist. This can be dangerous because a narcissistic can easily spot a potential victim and manipulate him/her by taking advantage of the fact that he/she might relate to them. The first sign that you might be in an abusive relationship is when your partner is always trying to get all the attention. When you don't pay any attention to him/her, they will use different strategies like creating drama or whatever it takes so you focus on them. A narcissist may be very jealous, controlling, and manipulative in an unhealthy manner.

A healthy relationship is one where both partners are well adjusted in a balanced manner. But when we start to recognize the signs of narcissistic behavior, it becomes easy to identify narcissistic traits. The signs to be aware of are:

1. Your partner is always trying to get your attention. This can be done through constant texting, calling you all the time, and even sending unwanted gifts that you don't need or want but are too polite or considerate to refuse.
2. Your partner has an over-inflated ego and characterizes himself/herself as a person who is intelligent and superior to most people in the world.

3. Your partner does not treat his/her victim with basic human respect and dignity. For example, if your partner insults you, he/she will never consider apologizing or making amends.
4. Your partner is condescending and superior in public but becomes very polite when alone with you.

In terms of relationships, narcissists thrive on control; they find it difficult to comprehend or accept that their victims have a definite opinion about certain issues. Therefore, it's normal that the victims be commanded to do certain things without being given any reason or explanation. They'll usually make abusive statements like, "When I shout you will do what I want," or "If you don't fall in line, nobody will love you." Narcissists tend to be possessive in relationships which can cause a lot of tension as they always think there's someone else whose attention is better than theirs.

One of the biggest issues people have with narcissism is that they feel as though they are being controlled by their partner rather than the other way round. While many might not see it as abuse, others would argue that while there is an element of control in most relationships, it shouldn't come across as abusive. While many people have the ability to be manipulative and controlling, it's the way that they go about it that is the biggest sign. This book will show you how not to get trapped in a relationship with a narcissist.

Narcissist is a word we come across almost every day, but what does it mean? In this book, we explored every point of it, and every angle was well researched to give you the best and well-compiled research on the subject. You may be struggling in your relationship, at home or with your friend and feel you are never enough. No matter how much you give it your best, you never really satisfy them, and you never reach the point they want you to. You feel like whatever you do is never good enough for them.

Well, this is the right book for you. You identify some characteristics of the typical narcissist, and now you will be able to understand the behaviors of some people and get to know why they do what they do. You may learn to accept the fact that you are not always the problem, but they are. Going deeper into this, you will know better how to handle such people. It might have been hard dealing with someone who demeans you all the time, is not able to understand you or even care what you are feeling.

You will know how to deal with a narcissist and live with them under the same roof without trying to please them. As wise man once said that at times, it is good to be a coward. When it comes a narcissist, you are actually not dealing with them at all, and you need to avoid these people at all costs. It's better to stick with others. We will give you some tips on how to prevent narcissist from entering your life or when you identify one, you know to run for your dear life before it is too late.

A narcissist can drain you and kill your self-esteem. to save yourself, stay away from them: that is the only way out. This will be a life-changing experience.

Chapter 1
What is Narcissistic Abuse?

N arcissists don't love themselves; they are driven by shame. It is an idealized picture they use to convince themselves that they embody what they admire. But deep down, a narcissistic feels a gap between the facade shown to the world and their ego-based shame. They work hard to prevent shame. This gap also applies to other offenders, but the narcissist uses defensive mechanisms that destroy normal conditions and cause pain and damage to the confidence of his loved ones. (To diagnose a narcissistic personality disorder, use "NPD").

Many narcissistic coping mechanisms are offensive; hence, the term "narcissistic abuse". However, someone can be abusive and not be a narcissist. Addicts and people with other mental disorders, such as bipolar disorder, antisocial personality disorder (sociopathy), and cross-border personality disorder are also abusive. Abuse is abuse, regardless of the diagnosis. If you're a victim of abuse, the biggest challenges are:

- Clear identification

- Building a support system

- Learn how to protect oneself

Abuse can be mental, physical, financial, spiritual or sexual. Here are some examples of abuse that you might not have detected:

Verbal violence: includes degradation, bullying, accusation, accusation, accusation, shame, demanding, orderly, threatening, criticizing, sarcasm, furious, averted, undermining, disrupting, blocking, and abusive. Note that many people sometimes use sarcasm, interrupt you, resist, criticize, blame or block. Consider the context, anger, and frequency of behavior before calling it narcissistic abuse.

Manipulation: generally affects someone who support self-centered and motivated goals. It often expresses a hidden aggression. Think of the "wolf in sheep's clothing". At first glance, the words appear harmless and they even complement each other; but underneath you feel humiliated or hostile. If your manipulation is entrenched, you may not recognize it as such.

Emotional extortion: include threats, anger, warnings, threats or punishment. It is a form of manipulation that casts doubt upon you. You feel a fear, duty and/or guilt, sometimes referred to as "FOG."

Gas Lighting: intentionally causes your suspicions to support your negative perception of reality or the belief that you are mentally incompetent.

Competition: competitive is high and insidious with a narcissist, sometimes with the use of unethical means. For example, cheating in a game.

Negative contrast: compare and contrasting you with narcissists or other people.

Sabotage: interfering with your efforts or relationships for revenge or personal gain.

Usage and objectification: using you for personal purposes regardless of your feelings or needs.

Recumbent: persistent scams without accountability or achieving the narcissist's goals.

Choice: things like money, sex, communication or love.

Ignoring : ignore the needs of a child for which the offender is responsible. Includes endangering children such as leaving a child in a potentially harmful situation.

Invasion of privacy: ignoring your personal borders by tracking you by phone or email; denying your physical privacy, chasing or follow you; ignoring the privacy you desire.

Character defamation: Spreading harmful gossip or lies about you to others.

Violence: blocking your movements, pulling you, throwing things, or destroying your property.

Financial abuse: includes controlling financial domination or emptying your finances by blackmailing, stealing, manipulating or gambling, or even creating debt in your name or selling your personal property.

Isolation: isolate you from friends, family, or access to external services and support through control, manipulation, verbal abuse, assassination, or other forms of abuse.

Malignant Narcissism and Sociopathy

A person with excessive narcissistic qualities who behaves harmfully and hostilely is considered to have "harmful narcissism". Harmful narcissists do not suffer guilt. They can be sadistic and enjoy causing pain. They can be so competitive and unprincipled that they exhibit anti-social behavior. Paranoia places them in a defensive attack mode as a means of self-defense.

Malignant narcissism is akin to sociopathy. Sociopaths have been crushed or damaged in some way so they exhibit narcissistic traits; but not all narcissists are sociopathic. Their motivations are different. While narcissists are ideal persons to be admired, sociopaths reach only for their self-sufficient agenda. They have to win at all costs and do not think about violating social norms and laws. They don't care about people like narcissists do.

Narcissists do not want to be abandoned. They depend on the approval of others, but sociopaths easily release relationships that do not serve them. Although some narcissists think about achieving their goals, they are usually more reactive than sociopaths who figure out their cold and evil plans.

You may have asked yourself at least a thousand times, "Why am I staying in this madness?" You may have come up with a possible answer - the fear of being alone - while acknowledging that your experience is not necessarily real fear itself. By assessing why you have remained in such an emotionally destructive relationship, you might conclude that although you prefer company; you also realize that discomfort and emotional pain come with the narcissist in your life.

You realize that you would be lonely by giving up this reality, and you distance yourself from grief to survive. You can experience, at least temporarily, some relief from emotional pain and discomfort. Yet it is unlike the emotional pain experienced by the narcissist who as an emotional addict and despite your efforts to attract their attention through various activities gets no relief.

You've found that you can be in the midst of your beloved family and friends, attend a long-awaited concert at a professional sporting event, go to a beautiful beach with perfect weather, yet have a broken heart. Unfortunately, you are unique in this experience. People advise, "Life continues. Come on. Stop apologizing. Don't give this person time to think about them. They certainly don't think about you." If all the well-meaning outsiders just knew how hard you have tried! Why are you going into this world of fear? Have you been told, "You must love pain because you are the one who chooses to stay with a narcissistic emotional addict?" It doesn't make sense to others, nor does it make sense to you.

You keep asking why? That's a good thing because only you can find the answer. Your journey is so unique. Will this curse ever be a blessing? If you survive, yes it will. The struggle, if you're still involved with a narcissistic emotional addict, is whether you want to survive. This does not mean that you are going to die, but it is also a possibility. What is being said here is that you existed before crossing paths with a narcissistic emotional abuser. You used to laugh, create, jump and run, smile and enjoy simple things in life. After joining a narcissistic r emotions, the colors, sounds, and smells of life have been lost to you. You live and breathe but feel dead inside, except for the pain stomach pain. Nothing makes more sense. You ask again, Why do I stay in this chaos? Why do I love them so much? Why do I love them more than my own life? Why? There is the possible joy of the "golden egg". Maybe they promises you to travel, own a house or build a bigger, nicer house. Do they have a lot of money? Does it make you feel like no friend has given you any similar feeling? When you are in their presence, no one else matters.

Think about it. What do they have on you? It's like a curse with an invisible power. You feel the curse attracting the narcissistic emotional abuser. It is like being in a prison cell with the door open, but you can't walk and stay outside. What kind of golden egg do they have? What did they do to make you start to believe that you can't live without them? They may deny this reality, even if you have clear evidence to support your case. Do you think somewhere in your mind that you are the winner of a revered golden goose if they choose you instead of all others?

Finding and understanding the golden egg with the narcissistic emotional culprit can be a challenge. Discovering your golden egg will reveal your most important uncertainties. This fear is so great in you that you risk death. You choose to endure abuse instead of dealing with it and making it become too real. It is said that most people die with the music that is still there. Do you have the courage to be yourself?

If you seek and find the golden egg with a narcissistic emotional abuser in your life, your curse will become a blessing. Be encouraged and dare to be you.

TYPES OF NARCISSISTS

Full-Blown Narcissist

A full-blown narcissist is the type that is not predictable nor preventable. These are types of people who strike when it is least expected, and nothing can be done to stop them. This is mainly characterized by an arrogance that disrupts and blows things out of proportion. Full-blown narcissism is the last stage where all the characteristics of narcissism have been blended and the victim, most of the time, turns out to be violent and uncontrollable. They can throw things everywhere or even mess because of a pure provocation at anything you do; a full-blown narcissist will always find a reason to get mad.

Covert Narcissist

A covert narcissist is the inverse of the overt narcissist in that they crave and demand self-importance and admiration, unlike the overt type who always needs to be right. Covert narcissistic behaviors are soft and subtle. Although they crave fame and recognition, they do it in ways that do not infringe another person's rights. The only difference between a covert and a full-blown narcissist is that the former chooses not to outwardly manifest their longing while the latter are fully intent on letting their demands known. In other words, coverts are an introverted version of full-blown narcissists although both fantasize about their self-worthiness and self-importance; the only difference is the way they manifest them. Many people have fallen victim of a covert narcissist because of the insidious way they work; you will never understand the harm they bring on their victims until much of it has been witnessed.

The primary characteristic of the overt narcissist is passive self-importance. They don't inflate their quest and thirst for admiration and importance, and they get them anyhow. Another trait of the covert narcissist is shaming others. Coverts never want to carry the blame, and they would rather shame and blame others for elevating themselves to be seen as of a higher caliber.

People With Narcissistic Tendencies

There are people who are narcissists, and there are people who are not narcissists but have narcissistic tendencies. One can manifest the traits of narcissists without being one. For instance, they can be self-centered with low empathy, and still they are not narcissists. So what qualifies one to be a narcissist, and what differentiates people with narcissistic traits from true narcissists?

People with narcissistic tendencies divide the populace into two: those to be looked up to and those to be looked down on. Unlike narcissists, people with narcissistic tendencies are realistic but instead have qualities worth emulating and others that are worth nothing.

The primary traits of people with narcissistic tendencies are domineering and always appear to know it all, but they will not be battling with self-esteem issues that the narcissists are fighting and grappling with. The only difference between the narcissists and people with narcissistic tendencies is that the people with tendencies have the capacity to see people as a mixture of good and evil and be able to associate themselves with the good ones while having nothing to do with the bad ones.

Narcissistic abuse is not exclusive. This kind of physical torment has happened to millions of people in the world. If it has happened to you too or is already happening to you now, know that you are not alone. You may be asking yourself, "Why me?" You might be feeling that this woeful experience is only happening to you. You might even blame yourself and feel like you are not good enough. But the truth is, you are not alone, and it is not your fault.

If you can, research about the experience you have been going through. Check on the internet about it. Take the next step and reach out for help. Talk to trusted people like professional counselors, experienced therapists, psychologists, friends, and family members that you can trust. You can even contact trauma facilities. Your healing will start immediately. You begin to see the reality of what has been happening to you. Seek help soon, especially if you are experiencing extreme symptoms like suicidal thoughts.

Make safety plans if you begin to see signs of people close to you becoming violent. In an abusive relationship, a trauma bond develops between the abuser and the abused. This is due to the hopelessness instilled in the abused person. However, sometimes moving and finding safety is less expensive than staying and taking in more abuse. It is possible to reach a point of recovery, with no or limited contact with the victim. The road to recovery is not easy, but it is worth it. The final destination will be attaining your freedom and getting yourself back on your feet.

In a nutshell, this is how narcissist abuse looks like: your happiness is denied, you lose your self-identity and have no freedom of expression. You are only there to listen and not to talk. You are to be seen not to heard. Your reality is warped and distorted. You are abused, threatened, manipulated, lied to, ridiculed, and taken through some ugly experiences. Then you are made to believe that you imagine things. You are called "mad" and told that you only have yourself to blame.

Perhaps you were even replaced and thrown out. Then you were lured back into the same cycle of abuse, this time with more painful experiences. You are stalked, harassed, and made to stay with the abuser by force. The most painful part is that the person doing all this to you is the very person who is supposed to protect you from it. It is the person you trusted and had hope in.

These are not the ups and downs of a healthy relationship no matter how much you might want to convince yourself that your companion is unique. This is an abusive companion who will break your soul, kill your sense of self, or even worse, your physical being. Other people will not understand, for you may not have physical scars to show. All you have are the internal wounds, fractured memories, and mental battles. This sounds very horrific. But don't be scared as it is possible to get yourself together. You can get your life back.

GETTING YOURSELF TOGETHER

Here are tips that will help you get yourself together.

Game Changing

Narcissists sabotage their victim's minds. They will make you believe that all that should matter to you is doing what they want without a second thought. Forget yourself and start singing songs of adoration to them. Sadly, no matter how much you give yourself to them, they are never satisfied. They get you on your toes at every moment. You keep thinking which of the next demands you should meet. Eventually, you bend to their desires. Don't get too involved in the narcissist monopoly conversations about what you have done wrong. Give yourself a break. tell yourself that it is not true. Detach fast and don't swallow that verbal poison.

Misrepresenting Your Thoughts and Words

Toxic narcissists perceive themselves as mind readers. They think they know what other people are thinking. They say things like, "I know you, I know what you want to say, I know how you think." They will put words into your mouth. They complete your sentences even before they begin. Also, before you get a chance to call out their misbehavior, they already are ready with excuses. You can only think about what they want you to believe, and you can only say what they want you to say. This is not good of course. The narcissist never evaluates what is really happening because they can't and won't come into terms with reality. They react to their triggers, created in their world of delusions.

State your case firmly and walk away with no more arguments. Do not give them a chance to shift the blame to you. The more you entrain them, the more they convince you that you should be ashamed of accusing them, and this could give them more rights to future abuse.

Changing the Subject

This is their common tactic. A narcissist will never want to be held accountable for any misdeed. They always redirect the conversation. The redirection often lands on one of the mistakes of the accuser. Narcissists are never afraid of pulling out your past mistakes, even if it committed ten years ago. They make it look so bad and render their accusers powerless by holding them accountable for everything. When this diversion happens, redirect it back to the original topic. State firmly that is not what you wanted to discuss. If they still insist on blaming you, stop the conversation and keep yourself busy with something else.

Smearing

A narcissist is capable of abusing deliberately so that you will react, and then they will use your reactions against you. They slander you and report back to anybody who cares to listen. They create stories to show that you are the abuser and they are the victim. Ironically, they accuse you of doing the wrong things they themselves do as a cover-up not to get the blame.

When this happens, seek help and avoid confrontation with the abuser. They will provoke and hurt you until you can't take it anymore. Then, they watch and wait for your reactions, which they will use against you. In case you seek justice, it is good to talk to a lawyer familiar with Narcissist Personality Disorder.

Triangulating

The narcissist may bring the views and opinions of other people into the dynamics of the relationship to validate their harmful actions and invalidate the reactions of their significant other. They triangulate them to parents, siblings, coworkers, strangers, and everyone else that matters. Triangulation can include love triangles. This influence other partners to use their opinions against you. This leaves you hanging, feeling insecure, and full of self-doubt. This is a tactic to disorient you from the toxic narcissist's behavior. It leads you to believe in their self-perception that they are desirable and perfect people. The narcissist also likes to report false information of what others say about you. This leaves you questioning yourself and feeling terrible about who you are.

To overcome triangulation, try your best to seek your validation. You can also reverse-triangulate a narcissist by gaining support from another person who is not influenced by the narcissist. The third party the narcissist is triangulating with is also triangulating with you. You are being played all around.

Preemptive Defense

A toxic narcissist likes to give themselves endless praise that has no basis. Despite having very dysfunctional behaviors, they want to show themselves up as a nice guy. Their conversations are full of boastful statements about how good they are and how other people should be associated with them. They overestimate their ability to be compassionate and kind.

These abusers expect everyone to see them as they see themselves. They cannot stand anybody who sees them as anything less than the right person. That is why their affinity for praise and affirmation never ends. They tell people to trust them even when they have not built a foundation for trust. Their false mask slips off as the abuse gets full brown and the cold and contemptuous personality is revealed. The victim becomes frustrated.

Your preemptive defense can be countered, so focus not on what the narcissist says, but what they do. Investigate why they insist on being a good person. You will find it is because they know you should not trust them, and they are afraid you will get to know this.

Sugarcoating

Malicious people find it fun to mess with others. They test and tease other people's mind then make it a joke. As discussed, narcissists are capable of squeezing your insecurities out of you, then document and use it in the future. They tell you something harmful to measure your reaction. They say they did not mean it and pretend to be innocent. This leaves you confused and vulnerable to future attacks. At this stage, you are being baited to stop being defensive altogether.

Your instincts can tell you when there are baiting and sugar coating. When they say something wrong and then ask you to take it lightly, that is a red flag. Do not listen to false flattery. Internalize what you feel about it and leave some space for detaching.

Being under the narcissist's manipulation is no joke. It is better to know how to counter them as early as possible. If you are already in it, take the first step. Be bold and seek all the help you can. If legal advice is required, do not hesitate to get it.

Chapter 2
How Narcissists Abuse

Many people are unaware of the abuse they suffer from a narcissist or just don't know that what they're going through is abuse because narcissistic abuse can be difficult to identify. Narcissistic behavior goes beyond being simply selfish and egocentric; it crosses into manipulation and brainwashing where the victim loses all sense of self-worth and independence.

Narcissists often spend time charming their victims while simultaneously criticizing them in private. They get you to invest your energy, emotions, and money in them then discard you without remorse when the relationship ends. It's a form of mental and emotional abuse that can leave the victim feeling confused, exhausted, and stressed. They may develop into Post-Traumatic Stress Disorder (PTSD) where depression, flashbacks and anxiety are not uncommon.

When someone is victimized by a narcissist for any length of time, it creates long-term effects on that person's life. The victim will have to suffer from the aftermath of narcissistic abuse for years after the relationship is over. They might spend years trying to make sense of what happened in their relationship with the narcissist, trying to understand how someone they loved so much could treat them so horrendously.

They might have to bury their feelings deep inside so as not upset other people around them. They might have low self-esteem, feel worthless or guilty, and blame themselves for the narcissist's abusive behavior.

It's normal for someone who suffered from narcissistic abuse to be confused and conflicted because they often idealized their abuser in the beginning of the relationship. They are reluctant to admit that the person they idolized is actually a dangerous abuser who has now completely shattered their self-esteem. Many victims think that they will be blamed by others when they start talking about how they were abused by a narcissist, so they keep quiet.

The following are ways in which narcissists abuse people:

Extreme Jealousy

The narcissist has an inverse sense of sexuality where they constantly feel inferior and jealous because they need constant admiration and attention to feed their fragile ego. They will often exhibit extreme paranoia about their partner's feelings for others, even if they have absolutely no reason to doubt them. If you are in a relationship with a narcissist, or had one in the past, then you probably remember countless late night fights because they got jealous over someone just trying to be friendly.

Using Guilt and Emotional Blackmail

The narcissist will use guilt, threats, and emotional blackmail to get what they want. The narcissist will accuse you of doing things that you probably didn't do (even though you wouldn't have done it if they hadn't asked). Narcissists know how to manipulate people by using fear and threats. They will also use guilt. You might have done something wrong in the narcissist's eyes, but they won't say anything directly; instead, they just accuse you of being a bad person and trying to escape them.

When you're in a relationship with a narcissist, you will often feel guilty like you're in the wrong. You might be feeling guilty about something they accused you of doing that you didn't do, or it could just be the way they accuse you of what is happening that makes you feel bad.

You might feel as though it was your fault for some reason, but the narcissist is the one who acted like a sociopathic child and has completely destroyed their partner's self-esteem. they continue to do so by assailing their partner with narcissistic rage. It's only normal to feel stressed when going through narcissistic abuse because it involves multiple forms of abuse all at once.

You may feel like everything you do is wrong, that you're a horrible person, and no one else would want to be with you. These are all normal feelings after being abused by a narcissist. The narcissist will do anything they can to make you feel guilty because it makes it easier for them to control you and keep you in the relationship.

Degradation and Humiliation

When you're in a relationship with a narcissist, you will feel small and worthless. You might even feel like you don't exist or your needs are unimportant. The narcissist will do anything to make sure that they feel superior to you in every way. They may constantly put you down or humiliate you in private by making jokes at your expense or by making fun of the things important to you.

Abusive Comments and Verbal Abuse

The narcissist won't say anything directly when they want to get their point across. It's all indirect, subtle, and oftentimes disguised as a joke or by making fun of you. If you start saying something, the narcissist might laugh at you because they know that will make you feel bad, and it makes it easier for them to control you.

The narcissist will find a way to make your life difficult without directly admitting it. They will use passive aggressive comments when they want to say something directly to piss you off without giving anything up in return. They have learned to never say anything in plain sight unless they want other people to know that they are being abusive towards their partner.

This also creates fear in the victim. They often cannot tell if they are being abused because they are so afraid of the consequences of it not working out. This is more common in people who haven't been abused before. Many times this abuse will come in the form of passive aggressive remarks or emotional abuse which can be harder to spot and prove.

Projection and Accusations

The narcissist will accuse you of things without actually saying anything directly to you. Of course, they will usually accuse you of doing things you probably didn't do, but it is equally likely they did do so as a way for them to exert control over your life.

Projective Identification and Provoking Defensiveness

The narcissist may start to make comments that are strange without really saying anything. They may accuse you of being a certain way or having certain traits that they actually have themselves. This is very common with abusive narcissistic relationships because the narcissist often has an extreme form of insecurity and feels that they need to prove their worth by destroying the other person instead of building a stronger relationship as a reciprocal exchange.

Engulfing, Entitlement, and Abusive Dependency

In this relationship dynamic, the narcissist will become so entwined in your life that it becomes difficult to live your own life. They will check up on you constantly and become the center of your life. They will oftentimes not leave you alone unless they think you are cheating on them or something else is wrong in your life.

They rarely give you your space. The narcissist wants to control what you do, who you are with, and what kind of friends you have. Even if it's not really that bad in their minds, they will often try to manipulate situations or people so it feels like everything is falling apart around them without actually doing anything bad themselves to make it happen.

Unreasonable Expectations of Reciprocity and Unpredictability

The narcissist is extremely unpredictable. They are very likely to do or say something that doesn't make any sense. They may give you gifts and be extremely kind and then turn around and talk about how much they hate you. This is because they feel entitled to have something when they want it, regardless of the fact that other people in their environment also exist on the same planet.

They will give you their attention when it suits them and then ignore you for days. They will demand a lot from their partners but not really give much in return. They will expect you to be on call for them 24/7 and have no problem making you feel like your life revolves around them.

Excessive Need for Admiration

Narcissists demand a lot of admiration and attention. They have a big "I'm the center of attention" mindset that can make it very difficult for their partners to get any attention or love from the other people in their lives. This means that they will likely become jealous if you friends, and they are not included in these relationships. They will get angry and upset if you take time doing things that don't involve them. That's a deal breaker for me.

And finally, the one thing that gets to me is when they talk bad about others behind their backs. Then I get really mad and upset. This is like cutting off your nose to spite your face. It's so stupid and shows a lack of respect. It is totally selfish and inconsiderate. Don't do it!

If you are married or in a committed relationship, only talk to your partner and other people in confidence or with full disclosure...it kills a friendship real fast when the person you are talking about finds out that you were talking behind their back.

When someone is narcissistic, it's easy to get sucked in. It seem like they are the only person you can count on. They will be very charming and personable with you in the beginning of the relationship because they want to seem like a person who values your friendship and interest.

This is usually when you become the victim of their manipulation and abuse. It might even take years for the full extent of it to hit home. It is very likely that you'll wake up one day and realize that you were deceived. You might be afraid to confront them because they are usually very good at making you feel guilty and that it's your fault you were abused.

The narcissist will use your emotions and heart against you. They will say things that make it seem like they care about you when they are actually just trying to get more control over your life to get what they want. If you are dating a narcissist, you need to walk away before they destroy your life. They will eat their way through your self-esteem and make sure that you never trust another person again.

Narcissistic abuse is extremely dangerous, and it is wise to walk away from the relationship. The forces of narcissism are scary, and if you let them get a hold of you, they will destroy your life. Your self-esteem won't be the only thing they will take. Chances are, they'll also destroy your sanity and self-worth. Please don't make the same mistakes I did and don't let a narcissist continue to abuse you.

Chapter 3
Gaslighting

N arcissists are absolute masters of manipulation. They can turn your whole life upside down in the blink of an eye. Unfortunately, what people don't often realize is that this abuse doesn't end there; it can continue for years after the relationship is over. This chapter will examine a common form of abuse from narcissists called gaslighting, which causes victims to second guess themselves and their perceptions.

Gaslighting is a form of emotional abuse where manipulators get in your head and convince you that what you know and see with your own eyes isn't real; it's all just happening in your head. This type of abuse is so effective because it happens gradually over time, making it very hard to notice that you're being manipulated.

What Does Gaslighting Look Like?

Gaslighting abuse manipulates memories, thoughts and emotions. It happens when someone says something that isn't true as if it is, but you are so confused that you begin second-guessing yourself. One common tactic the narcissist uses to gaslight his victims is called "blanking" the victim. This means that at certain points, the narcissist will try to erase a person from their memory or pretend like they never existed; this includes pretending like certain events or conversations never happened. This type of gaslighting can be especially damaging because the narcissist is essentially denying his partner's reality.

Gaslighting also includes twisting a victim's perception of their own reality. One obvious form is lying to someone, but it can be much more subtle than that. Let's say both David and Brandi are at home in their apartment when Jane, who they know, comes to the door to drop something off as she often does.

In this situation, Brandi has answered the door and is startled to see Jane there; she thought she was alone with David who is reading. Now Jane walks in and sees David reading a book instead of being on his computer as he usually is at this time of the day. Jane questions David and asks him what he is doing. David says he was doing some research for work, which is true. However, Brandi heard this and thought to herself, Really? He's telling Jane that he was doing research for work when he said only thirty minutes ago he said that he was going to take a break from the computer to read? This is where things get tricky. Brandi continues to have doubts about David's claims even though they were all true.

The most extreme form of gaslighting can potentially cause the victim to start questioning their own sanity, making them think that they themselves are crazy. Gaslighting is one of the most toxic forms of emotional abuse because it so completely infects your reality. It takes a lot of strength to stand up to this type of manipulation because you have to convince yourself that what you know and see with your own two eyes really happened. If you begin to doubt yourself, it makes it easier for the manipulator to get away with his or her abuse.

How Does Gaslighting Happen?

Gaslighting abuse isn't just a one-time occurrence; it happens over an extended period of time and gives the abuser the chance to manipulate his or her victim over and over again. It starts by slowly gaining trust to access the partner's life. Once she has gained access, she begins to slowly confuse and manipulate the victim over time. The gaslighting abuser changes their stories, contradicts themselves, and twists reality to make it sound like the victim is delusional.

The abuser also starts other arguments to deflect attention away from their own lies. At this point, the victim begins to have doubts about themselves and what they believe is real, which causes them to question their own reality. The manipulator then uses these doubts against the victim while continuing the abuse.

How to Deal with Gaslighting

There are three main ways to deal with gaslighting. The first is not to be controlled by it because when you are gaslighted, you are essentially being controlled by the abuser. You are not in control of yourself, making it extremely difficult to escape the situation. The second way is to learn how to recognize the signs and tell people what's going on. This will make it easier for your friends and family members see what is happening. The third way is to have a support system in place while confronting your abuser; it's hard enough to deal with an abusive relationship without support from those around you.

How to Deal with Your Own Doubts

In every abusive situation, the victim becomes the person they're trying to escape. They lose their identity, and they don't know themselves anymore. This is why it's so important to take time for yourself to get back in touch with who you really are. Don't let someone else define you - it's your life. Take some time for yourself and reflect on what you want and need out of life; this will help you rediscover parts of yourself that may have gotten lost in the abuse. If any part of your identity has been tainted by gaslighting, it's time to put it behind you.

Recovery

If you're the victim of gaslighting abuse, don't give up. It's so important to remember that there is no such thing as a perfect relationship; if you have one, then it's not yours. Your partner should support and help you grow into your best self and not manipulate you into believing what they think is real.

If your relationship feels like it's impossible to break out of, then reach out for help. You do not have to face it alone; there are many resources that can help you along your journey to freedom. You are worth the fight, and no one has the right to deny your reality but you.

Gaslighting can happen to anyone regardless of gender, age or position. However, it is a well-known fact that women are more prone to this type of abuse than men, and the three most common types of gaslighters are parents, siblings and partners. Older women (50–85 years) experience the highest rates of physical and sexual violence from younger male partners in intimate relationships when they are also experiencing ageism.

Gaslighting may be described as an extreme case of emotional abuse by manipulation. The abuser wants the victim to question their own feelings, instincts, and sanity by distorting the truth. Gaslighting abuse is often subtle. Its victims are led to question their own reactions through "family" or "friend" manipulation, usually portrayed as a joke, which can lead to anxiety, depression, and ultimately substance abuse problems. These can be the more severe manifestations of the abuse.

The victims of gaslighting don't recognize it as an act of violence until they have been deceived for so long that their former reality is distorted, and they think the new reality truly exists. This is often the reason why a victim doesn't come forward because they feel certain that no one would believe them.

The abuser also manages to make the victim's situation seem more critical than it actually is, which causes emotional distress. It is no wonder that the victim is more prone to using substances to cope with their situation or escape. Many abusers have even been known to exploit their victim's substance abuse problems for financial gain.

Chapter 4
Narcissist Target: Traits that Makes You a Prime Target for Narcissists

F irst, it is important to note that the popular notion that narcissists target weak, desperate women or men is nothing short of misleading. Also, being a victim of narcissistic abuse is never the victim's fault by any means. Narcissists are emotional predators and the fact that you're a human makes you automatically vulnerable to their antics. That said, it makes sense to identify the traits that narcissists identify in their targets so that potential victims can better protect themselves and sever ties early on, especially when they realize they are being targeted for exploitation.

When you consider these traits, you'll realize how wonderful they are, especially if allowed to blossom in a healthy and loving relationship. Sadly, a narcissist will only use them to manipulate, exploit ,and damage their victims. Below are some of the traits that narcissists look out for in potential victims:

1. Conscientiousness

2. Empathy

3. Integrity

4. Resilience

5. A high degree of sentimentality

6. Conscientiousness

Many people do not realize this, but one of the prime qualities a narcissist looks for is the ability of the potential victim to be conscientious. Truth be told, conscientious people are always concerned about the wellbeing of others, and they always carry out their obligation. The reason they are vulnerable to narcissists is that their decisions are tied to their conscience and, sadly, they project their sense of morality onto the narcissist, assuming that he will do the same.

Narcissists are very manipulative; they know how easy it is to exploit people who are conscientious enough to worry about other people's needs. They know that a conscientious person is one of the very few people that would grant them numerous chances, give them benefit of doubt, and even care more about them than their personal needs.

Narcissists love to target conscientious people for romantic relationships because they are aware of the fact that conscientious people see caretaking as an obligation, especially in relationships. They know that these people are ready to fulfill their obligations even if they feel endangered or if it puts them in harm's way.

Dr. George Simon, in his book, Personalities Prone to Narcissistic Manipulation, said that disturbed individuals most often target those who possess two qualities that they, themselves, don't possess. These traits are excessive agreeableness being very conscientious. People with these traits tend to defer to others, such as the narcissist, by complying with their demands and manipulation. Ironically, those who possess a conscience are more vulnerable to those who do not. Shame and guilt are the primary tools or weapons used by those who manipulate others, but in order for that to work, you have to have the capacity for these traits in the first place.

Empathy

The joy of every narcissist is to encounter an empathic victim because narcissists, in general, do not get a constant narcissistic supply of attention, praise, resources, etc. from people who lack empathy - like themselves. Thus, the importance of securing a narcissistic target cannot be overemphasized.

Narcissists cannot show empathy towards others, but they carefully target people who have a great deal. The physical and emotional validation that empathic people give narcissists help maintain their bloated egos and feelings of authority, or else they practically starve and renew their hunt for a new source of supply.

When you put everything into consideration, you'll realize that empathic people are the opposite of narcissists, and their attitude helps to empower narcissists in their abuse cycle. For example, the fact that an empath is always willing to see the narcissist's perspective even at the height of abuse is something that maintains the abuse cycle over and over. As if that is not enough, narcissists identify with empathic people because they know that they're the ideal audience for their pity ploys even after highly abusive incidents.

If you happen to be an empathic person, understand that narcissists believe they can just put out a faux apology or sob story to write off their abuse. They know you'll always see reasons for their toxic behaviors and even make excuses on their behalf. They depend on your God-given ability to forgive and sympathize with them irrespective of the ill treatments they've subjected you to in the past.

Most times, narcissists escape retribution and accountability for their actions because they appeal to the empathy of their victims. It is very hard to pretend to be who you are not, and as such, empathic people, being who they are, always second-guess their decisions to punish the narcissists for their actions because they feel an unbearable amount of guilt when they see the narcissist prosecuted (either by society or law). Thus, they are always inclined to protect their abusers as opposed to exposing them to the world as to who they truly are.

Integrity

This might sound very funny, but narcissists are incredibly attracted to people who keep to their word. When they come in contact with people of integrity, they see a lot of attributes they can exploit for their own gain. For example, if it is not in the moral code of a victim to cheat or give up on a relationship prematurely, who stands to benefit? The narcissist, who is morally and mentally impoverished!

While the victims feel morally apprehensive about betraying the relationship, executing retaliation, or even withdrawing from their supposed obligations to the narcissists, the narcissist in question maintains zero remorse for harming their victims. The victim possesses a rare gift that can be of benefit to them and their partners in a healthy and productive relationship. However, this same gift becomes a weapon in the hands of a narcissist – a deadly weapon used to destroy their self-worth and self-belief.

Resilience

The most painful part about being a victim of narcissistic abuse is the realization that you weren't even wrong most times. As a victim of narcissistic abuse, your ability to bounce back from your abuser's acts is something that strengthens your bond with him. Resilient people, e.g. childhood abuse survivors, are highly effective sources for the narcissist because they have a very high threshold for pain and abuse.

Resilience is a very good quality to possess, especially when faced with adversities of life, but in an abusive relationship, the victim's resilience is exploited and used against him/her to keep them enslaved in the abuser's web of deceit and manipulation.

Even though resilient people are more aware of the dangers of their environments, they still find it difficult to give up on their abusers even after multiple incidents. Typically, they will choose to disregard their instincts and fight for their relationship by assuming the role of a "fighter" or "savior," as they put in energy to keep an unsustainable relationship afloat.

The saddest part about the resilient victim is that there are times when they even quantify their love by the amount of abuse they've suffered at the hands of their abusers. Unknown to them, this occurs because they have successfully developed an abuse bond with the toxic and abusive partner.

High degree of sentimentality

There is no gainsaying that narcissists are overbearing, petty, and manipulative. Thus, targets who are sentimental and capable of falling deeply in love, are extremely appealing to narcissists because they know they can use love-bombing (the use of extreme praise and flattery to groom a victim) to easily manipulate them.

During the early stages of narcissistic relationships, narcissists shower their victims with so much love and attention: the idea is to secure their trust and appeal to their craving for love. It is a strategy that works very well for them! They intentionally create sweet memories that they want their victims to romanticize during future periods of abuse.

Narcissists love to play with their victim's emotions; they know they can get their victims hooked before they start to withdraw by creating a fraudulent "soulmate" effect that will cripple their victims and leave them wanting things to be as they were during the early stages of the relationship.

Narcissists find it very easy to trick empathic and sentimental people – the only thing they do is fraud their victims into believing they're kicking off a meaningful, long-term relationship. It is very normal for people to want to maintain long term, healthy relationships, but it becomes a problem when a predatory narcissist is involved.

Why did the narcissist target you? You have something the narcissist wants (lifestyle, power, money, position). In a narcissistic relationship, certain things come into play. First of all, it begins with a hook – a dream – and most times you think it is all about you and your wellbeing, but the truth is that the narcissist is all about control.

There are occasions when the narcissist will appear to be helpful, but when things don't go as planned, the tables turn on you. However, when you realize the pattern and opt to hold the narcissist accountable for his actions, things get out of hands and degenerate rapidly.

Chapter 5
Coping with a Narcissist

B eing able to identify a narcissist is just the beginning. Once you recognize that you have one in your life, the next step is knowing how to overcome the experience and its associated consequences. It can be emotionally and mentally challenging to be around a person with narcissism. It is imperative not to delay dealing with the situation properly to minimize potential negative effects.

Dealing with a Narcissist

Dealing with a narcissist is something that truly takes practice. It takes a different tack than those without narcissism, and since this is not an issue you deal with frequently with multiple people, there is a learning curve. Never discount yourself. This is what they want, but there are ways to ensure that you are creating and maintaining the right boundaries.

Do Not Give in to Their Fantasy

A narcissist builds a fantasy life, and when dealing with them, it is important not to fall into the fantasy. They can be charming so it can be hard to resist them. It does not take long to essentially get lost in their web. At first, you might feel important and special, but this never lasts. Keep the following in mind:

- They will not fulfill your needs. In fact, what you need and want will not even be recognized. A narcissist views your value as what you can do to satiate their ego.

- Pay attention to how they treat others. You will see that they are not afraid to manipulate, lie, disrespect and hurt other people. Eventually, this behavior and treatment will trickle down to you.

- While it is not easy, the rose-colored glasses have to come off to evaluate how they are truly treating you. When you care about someone, denial is the easiest route to take concerning their true character, but this has to be put aside.

- Don't forget about your dreams. When you are close to a narcissist, it is easy to get swept up in their delusions and fantasy. Do not lose yourself or you may find it hard to regain control.

Set Boundaries and Stick to Them

One of the biggest elements of a healthy relationship is setting healthy boundaries and sticking to them. Of course, a narcissist does not understand boundaries, so this can be tricky. Remember that your relationships with others should be built on a foundation of mutual respect and care. While you will not get what you give, you still have to approach the relationship like any other. This will reduce the chances of your boundaries being violated.

For example, a narcissist is not shy about taking what they want. You might have a female friend who is a narcissist who just raids your closet and takes anything at any time. In a normal friendship, this friend would ask first, but narcissists do not ask permission. They feel they deserve anything they want, and this includes anything you have.

If you have had a relationship with a narcissist for a while, you surely can see their pattern of not respecting boundaries. To change this, make a plan based on what you hope to achieve. Then, consider how you will enforce the plan and what the consequences will be should the narcissist violate your boundaries. The most important thing is that you stand firm and do not give into the needs of the narcissist. Let them know when your boundaries have been crossed.

Be prepared for relationship changes. A narcissist is not a big fan of people who don't admire them and give into their every whim. They want to call all the shots, and they want you to prop them up. Once you start creating boundaries, how they treat you is likely to change because they will not be happy about you standing up for yourself.

They may try to punish you, demean you, or go in the opposite direction and use fake charm to manipulate you into going back to giving them what they want. To maintain the friendship, you might take a gentle approach to boundary setting. For example, instead of just abruptly changing things and being harsh when explaining why, plan what to say and then deliver the message in a way that is clear, calm, gentle and respectful. If the conversation is not going as planned, simply walk away. Do not continue to engage or allow the person to try and manipulate you into going back to your old habits of giving in.

Avoid Taking Things Personally

This will be one of the hardest things you do, but it is important. A narcissist is not purposely trying to hurt you. This is just who they are, and they are unable to see fault in their behavior. Remember that their actions, behaviors, and emotions are not about you. It is all about them.

A narcissist will try and create a version of you that is easiest for them to control. Work on your self-esteem and know your worth so their view of you does not become how you see yourself. Let them keep their own negativity and do not allow it to change how you feel about yourself.

This also means that you need to know who you are. A narcissist is not able to admit that they have weaknesses, and they overinflate their strengths. However, you need to take an honest look at yourself. If a narcissist is attacking one of your strengths, you can simply walk away. You know it is something you are good at. Be proud of it and do not allow them to make you feel inferior.

Do not argue with them. This will be hard when the natural instinct is to defend yourself when someone is attacking you. Remember that a narcissist is not rational and no amount of logic will change this. Simply state calmly that you disagree and then walk away.

Lastly, never look to a narcissist for approval. Even if they tell you nice things, they are only doing it to manipulate and gain control over you. As long as you know your worth and have good self-esteem, you do not need them to approve of anything you do or think.

Find a Good Support System

A narcissist is never going to be a good support person for you. However, you do need support when dealing with someone like this in your life. If they are close to you and have been in your life a while, the first step is learning what a healthy relationship is. It is about mutual respect and give and take. With a narcissist, you only give, and they only take.

Focus your time on those who give you love, respect, and honesty. This will help you to see who you truly are so you do not have to get approval from the narcissist in your life. Start to break away. A narcissist wants all attention, so they often isolate those they want to keep for themselves. This makes it easier for them to gain control over you. Spend time meeting new people or reconnecting with friends you might have lost touch with.

Seek out meaningful opportunities and activities. Consider going for that promotion you have wanted, volunteer, or try a new hobby. When you have a fulfilling life, its acts as a natural support system.

How to Treat a Narcissist

You want to start by distinguishing between a grandiose narcissist and a vulnerable one. When you are dealing with one that is vulnerable, they have a weak inner core they are masking with outward self-absorption and self-centeredness. The grandiose ones are not shy about how great they believe they are, and they truly believe they are the best.

Treating a narcissist in the right way is the easiest method to ensure that their negative behavior does not fall back on you and cause negativity in your life. To ensure that you are treating them in the right way, there are a number of things to do so you can evaluate them and develop the best strategy.

Determine the Narcissist's Type

You want to know if you are dealing with a vulnerable or grandiose narcissist. This makes it possible to determine what is needed to get the best response from them. For example, the grandiose type feels they are the best, so they need their ego stroked. On the other hand, the vulnerable type needs to feel special at all times due to their fragile ego. They need constant praise and reassurance.

Acknowledge How Annoyed You Are

Narcissists can really get into your skin, causing you to be annoyed with them. They want all of the attention, so they commonly interrupt you when you are doing anything other than giving them attention. Do not just blow this off. Instead, acknowledge that their behavior annoys you so you can start putting a stop to it.

Consider the Context

In many cases, certain situations trigger the worst narcissistic behavior. For example, you have a coworker who desperately wanted a promotion, but someone else got it. If she is a narcissist, this rejection may cause her to become very insecure, and in some cases, angry. This would result in her becoming spiteful, vindictive and downright difficult to deal with.

Know the Source of the Behavior

A narcissist does not think like everyone else. For those without narcissism, getting over insecurities is not overly difficult. It is just part of healthy coping. However, with a narcissist, they essentially need to have their ego rebuilt after a situation that caused them to feel inferior. It is important to balance how you treat them after a tough time.

For example, you are working on a school project with someone who is a narcissist. Something happens that exposes a weakness. This breaks their ego and can make them just stop working on the project, but you still need their contribution. To get them back on track, give them balanced reassurance. Too much and their ego can quickly get too big again, so approach the situation with this in mind.

Do Not Allow the Narcissist to Derail You

When you are doing something that takes attention away from them, they might try to sabotage you so that you stop doing it and get back to making them number one. It is important that you keep your goal upfront and do not allow anything they do or say to stop you from pursuing your goal or doing what you want to do.

For example, you and the narcissist usually do something together on Friday nights. However, you decide you want to start taking a class on your own. Since this takes your attention away from them, they may try to do things to get you to quit taking your class. Do not give in.

Make Sure to Stay Positive

Narcissists feed on watching other people feel bad, so even if they cause you to experience negative emotions, do not let them see this. When you are around them, make sure you are in a positive mindset. No matter how hard they try to bring you down, keep a smile on your face and do not react.

Call Their Bluff

Remember that the narcissist wants to keep you down because this makes it easier for them to control you. When they are trying to do something negative, do not give in and do not get offended. Instead, walk away or laugh. They want to see you upset, so if you do not do this in front of them, it starts to take away some of their control.

Know That They Need Help

Narcissism is a mental health issue that someone cannot just be willed away. They will need help if they ever expect to get their behavior under control. If you approach them and recommend they reach out to a professional, they are unlikely to agree and go. They may even become angry or defensive. If you care about the person and want them to at least consider help, approach the subject gently and know that this is something you will likely have to discuss several times before they will even consider it.

Freeing Yourself from Negative Emotions

Anger, jealousy, envy and other negative emotions can permeate your life and cause significant problems. It is important to recognize their existence and then work to be free of them. Freeing yourself from such emotions is a process, and it takes time. Even after you free yourself, you will need to commit to long-term work and maintenance.

Negative emotions are powerful and can quickly become habits if you do not get them under control. For example, if you commonly respond to criticism with anger, over time, this repetition will cause you to become angry any time you are criticized. This can start to impact your relationships, your career, and other elements of your life.

Stop Justifying

Stop justifying your negative emotions. If you are getting angry all of the time, take responsibility for why and stop trying to place the blame elsewhere. Anger is a very powerful emotion that can quickly become a habit. As soon as you recognize that this habit is problematic and admit it is not good, you can start to reevaluate why you are feeling this way so you can change it.

Stop Making Excuses

When you make excuses for negative emotions, either for yourself or others, you are telling yourself that they are out of your control. This is not true because you have the choice as to how you react to a situation. If you continue to make excuses, you will never take responsibility for your behavior. Over time, this can start to push people out of your life because they will not want to be around someone who cannot admit their faults or when they are wrong.

Take Responsibility

Once you dedicate yourself to no longer making excuses, you can start to take some responsibility for how you act in various situations. This starts by taking the power away from your negative emotions. As you continue to take responsibility, you will find that they lose their hold over you. The right reactions and choices will naturally start to become easier to make.

Do Not Overanalyze Other People's Opinions of You

Your emotions are your responsibility, but external factors can make them a bit harder to control. One of the biggest external factors is how other people view you. This is especially true if someone is especially vocal in criticizing you. This is often what narcissists do to keep you under their control.

Humans naturally want to be wanted and loved. When someone you respect or care about says something negative about you, the natural reaction is to go on the offensive. However, you want to instead hear what they are saying and then determine if it is true.

For example, did your supervisor yell at you for making a small error on a work project? Consider why they yelled. Think about the big picture. Okay, you made a small mistake, but overall, you completed the project and did well with it. Remember this and allow the yelling to roll off your back.

Stop Your Bad Habits

Any bad habit you have can add to the negatively in your life. For example, eating fast food often, smoking or not maintaining good dental hygiene. Take time to write down your bad habits. Once you put them in writing, they are easier to recognize. Start by working on one at a time because it is easier to correct a bad habit when you put a lot of focus on it. When you work to enhance your total wellbeing, your emotions will benefit.

Cut Off Negative People

If people in your life are largely a negative influence, walk away. It does not matter how close you are or how long you have known the person. When they are constantly negative, this is not doing any good for your life. If you really care about the person, you can consider talking to them. However, not everyone can change, and some may just not want to. For example, a narcissist is not able to just stop their negative behavior. It is a part of their personality. Because of this, simply talking to them is not likely to get you anywhere.

Think Before Responding

Negative emotions are powerful, so it is not uncommon for them to spill out. However, train yourself to wait 10 seconds before responding to a situation that causes negative emotions. This allows you to calm down so your response is appropriate for the situation. For example, you were supposed to meet a friend for dinner, and you were an hour late. They are upset. Instead of just responding back in anger and getting into a fight, count to 10 and then consider why they are mad. It will be easier to see that they did nothing wrong and you should apologize.

Be Grateful

Even during the worst of times, you have awesome things in your life that you should be grateful for. When you put your focus on them, it helps to alleviate the negative feelings. Consider keeping a journal and at the end of each day, take a few minutes to write down all the good things that happened that day. Over time, the positive elements of your life will start to naturally outweigh the negative.

Stop Saying, "I Can't"

If you keep telling yourself that you cannot do something, you will eventually start to believe it. This is what is referred to as a self-fulfilling prophecy. Give yourself credit and stop limiting yourself to what is easy and in your comfort zone. As you push yourself and see how many things you are truly good at, it will put you in a more positive frame of mind, naturally pushing out the negative emotions.

Let It Go

Life would be much simpler if everything could be controlled, but this is not possible. When you find something you have no control over, recognize it and let it go. For example, not every person will like you, and there are times when a loved one may get mad at you for something that is not your fault. Do not press the issue. Let go, and everything will eventually work itself out.

There are simple things you can start doing on a regular basis to push out negative emotions and enhance your overall wellbeing. You do not have to do every single one on a daily basis but consider them and incorporate some into your day when appropriate.

- Be proactive and do not allow the negative to settle into your life

- When life gets tough, cry it out because this aids in reducing stress

- Scream as loud as you can for a few seconds as this naturally counteracts negative emotions

- Get some sleep since it is easier to tackle stress and negative emotions when you are not exhausted

- Try to be positive and no matter what happens, force yourself to find the silver lining in the situation

- Take a few minutes to laugh every day since when you are laughing, negative emotions cannot be present

- Find someone you trust who cares about you and talk to them when you need to get help with a problem

- Consider an alternate perspective to see if it might allow you to better solve a problem

- Forgive yourself for setbacks as long as you recognize them and do not allow them to completely throw you off track

- Own your feelings and when negative emotions occur, recognize them, consider why you are experiencing them, and then detach from it

- Write about the day or experience you just had before going to bed each night as this allows you to leave the negative in the past so you can start fresh the next day

Chapter 6
Surviving Narcissistic Abuse

N o matter how a relationship of this nature has put you down or worn you out, you can rise again. Despite the abuse and strife and all the mind games, you can come out strong and regain your sanity. Narcissism exists in different phases of life relationships. It is not only peculiar to romantic relationships; narcissism exists in business and at work, among families, siblings, and friends. But before we explore this, we should talk about the psychological effects of narcissism on its victims.

Impact of Narcissism on the Brain

Many people find themselves stuck in abusive relationships. It could be emotionally abusive parents, a friendship or romantic relationship. The effect is almost the same, which is more than mere emotional and physiological damage. Neuroscientists have revealed that narcissistic abuse can cause physical brain damage in victims.

When exposed to emotional trauma for an extended period, it can trigger symptoms of PTSD. This is why the remedy for abusive relationships is to leave. Walk away before you lose your entire self to this person. Unknown to many, the long-term effect of narcissism is way more than emotional and psychological distress.

What many do not know is that the brain is actually damaged by regular exposure to emotional abuse. With this prolonged exposure to abuse, the amygdala can swell and some experience a reduction in the size of the hippocampus (Morey, 2012.) The after-effect of this is horrible, but to understand why, we must understand the role of the amygdala and hippocampus.

The amygdala is responsible for negative emotions such as fear, anxiety, worry, guilt, and shame. The hippocampus helps in the formation of memories as well as learning. To effectively learn as humans, we should be able to retain information into our short-term memory. This is the first step in learning. This needs to happen before any information gets transferred to long-term memory. In other words, short-term memory is as crucial to learning as long-term memory.

Damage to the hippocampus produces a devastating effect. According to a study at the University of New Orleans and Stanford University, a reduction of the hippocampus is linked to high levels of cortisol (a stress hormone) in the body (Carrion, 2007.) In other words, excess stress in people makes the hippocampus smaller.

The amygdala, known as the reptilian brain, is in charge of emotions such as fear, hate, lust, etc. It is also related to breathing and heart rate. It is responsible for triggering the fight and flight response. Victims of narcissistic abuse are always in a state where their amygdala is on high alert. With time, these people transition to a state where fear and anxiety become a constant, and the amygdala will pick up on the slightest sign of abuse.

Even after the victim has left the abusive relationship, there are lingering signs of post-traumatic stress such as panic attacks and excessive phobias. This is because the amygdala's increased size now considers the state of fear and anxiety as normal. To try and keep themselves from the reality of the situation, victims use reality twisting devices such as:

Projection: in a bid to try and deny the facts, victims choose to believe that the narcissist is not all bad. They want to believe deep down that there is some compassion. Most of the time, this is a lie.

Denial: victims refuse to accept the gravity of their situation. They convince themselves that living with it is better than any confrontation.

Compartmentalization: victims ignore the abusive aspects of the relationship and choose to focus only on the positive ones.

The Gradual Damage of the Hippocampus

The hippocampus helps us read, study, understand, and process information. In other words, the hippocampus handles everything related to learning and knowledge. Since it relates to learning, it is associated with the formation of new memories.

This crucial part of the brain is negatively affected by stress due to the presence of cortisol. Cortisol decreases the size of the hippocampus, making us more subjected to stress and anxiety. The more these distressing emotions thrive in the brain, the more our brain is changed.

Stress from narcissistic abuse, both of a short and long-term stress duration, are equally damaging. As a result, even subtle abuse and manipulation from the abuser can destroy the victim's brain. With many methods of healing available to those who experience abuse, you can reconfigure the brain to have a normal reaction to stress.

Surviving Narcissistic Abuse in Families

Do either of these scenarios sound familiar?

- A mother tells her daughter that no man will want her if she is fat
- A father lies to his children and dismisses their opinions, all to get them to do things for him

Some level of narcissism is prevalent in most families. There are many tactics a narcissist's parents could choose to exert control over their children. This often has a profound effect on the child, creating deep and painful wounds on the child's mental state. Being raised by a narcissistic parent can be devastating and potentially degenerating, causing low self-esteem if left unaddressed by the adult.

Naturally, it is believed that love should be instilled in all parents. There should be this unbroken bond that connects parents to their children. Looking specifically at the kind of intimacy a child shares with the mother, you expect to find an unbreakable chord of love that brings them together. However, not every mother is capable of unconditional love.

Some parents have been so eaten away by their past traumas that they don't see their children as special human beings deserving of their love. Instead, these parents only see them as extensions of themselves. This explains why they perceive their children as competition, a source of jealousy, and sometimes even a threat.

To narcissistic parents, their youngsters are objects that hinder their personal needs. Being raised by a narcissistic parent can be devastating for a child. However, healing is possible as soon as the child realizes it's important. You don't need to spend a lifetime trying to mend your broken and damaged self-esteem due to your parents. To heal, you have to:

Mourn: you were robbed of the normal childhood every kid deserves. Remember this and mourn properly as you would when losing something important.

Accept: you see another child's mother and wish yours was like her. You need to accept that your life is just different from others, and that's okay. Your upbringing has little to do with you; it was just an unfortunate turn to be born into a broken home, devoid of love and normal human emotions. You need to accept that this is who your parents were and make the best of it.

The process of grieving and accepting is primal to healing. This is not about healing the relationship with your parents but the relationship with yourself. Continuous exposure to abuse or neglect from your parents may have eroded your self-esteem, lowered your confidence, or made you feel unworthy of love, but there's always a chance to improve. The love, care, and attention you never received from your parents can instead come from you.

Other healing techniques are:

Get Rid of Your Inner Critic

During the abuse while with your parents, you believed they might love and accept you if you were more talented or smarter. When this never happened, you resolved that you were clearly unlovable. This left the voices of your parents in your head always criticizing and being negative. Allowing behavior like this to continue will only start a cycle of shame and abuse. Be kind to yourself and understand that no one is perfect.

Embrace Your Inner Child

You may think blocking it out is the way to cope. Nope. Think deeply about your feelings at this time. Look inward and see yourself when you were criticized and felt unloved. Embrace this helpless child and develop a strong, safe, loving relationship with that person - it is you after all. Rather than constantly criticizing yourself, try to see your flaws in a different way. With warmth and acceptance, embrace this poor damaged kid with compassion.

Exercise Self-Care

Living and growing up with narcissistic parents might have conditioned you not to focus on your needs. You only seek to please and do what you think makes them happy. As a result, you are completely lost on how to embrace your needs.

Fix this by treating yourself. Do something just for you and spend time alone to really begin to love for yourself, maybe an activity or adventure that makes you nothing but happy. You and your needs matter. Considering that a child spends an average of fifteen years living under the pressure of a parent, with narcissists, that time might feel like an eternity. Abuse doesn't happen overnight or over the span of a year, so the journey to recovery can be long and at times hard. Good things take time, so allow yourself to take the time you need while being surrounded by people you love. In time, you will see visible improvements in every aspect of your life; developing a healthy and loving relationship with yourself and others are just the baby steps you need to begin.

Healing Narcissistic Abuse in Relationships

Suffering mental, physical, and emotional abuse at the hands of a narcissist can be one of the most challenging things to get through. It affects every part of the victim's life, eroding their confidence and making them doubt themselves. Constant attacks with no relief or time for the mind and body to process the attack, let alone heal, is why many people end up with symptoms of PTSD.

The following steps can help the healing begin:

Create Ironclad Boundaries

To heal yourself from an abusive relationship, you need an imaginary barricade to keep the negativity out, in the form of boundaries. This is the foundation for your healing journey to get off the ground. Thinking you're out of the fray leaves you vulnerable to the narcissist, potentially giving them another chance to mess with your head. This contact can trigger pain that can pose as a major setback.

While the best method is to physically stay away from them, you can also give them the cold shoulder or just ignore them if getting away isn't easy. Leave no opportunity for them to prey on your emotions. Be emotionally distant even while interacting with them. You also need to learn object. This is a gradual way to build your self-esteem and regain your confidence.

Forgive Yourself

Some part of you knew all along that something was not right, but you were so drunk in love you didn't realize. This can make you shoulder the blame and be too hard on yourself. This won't help. Anybody could have been the victim, you were just in the right position to get in bed with a broken person. You were manipulated, tricked, and brainwashed. You could not have seen it coming even if there were a ton of warning signs. Realize that you are a whole person, full of love and deserving of love.

You are kind, smart, and worthy. It is the narcissist's loss for not knowing your true worth.

Adjust Your Focus

Having spent a lot of time with your abuser, there will an overload of moments to reflect on. This is a trauma bond—a sign that there are unprocessed emotions you need to deal with. The idea here is to find time to work on them with mindful intention, rather than being dragged by your past forever. Embrace mindfulness and engage in visualizations of a bright and hopeful future.

The narcissist may have made you bench your dreams for theirs, but it's time for you to start working on them again. With a revitalized sense of purpose, you can get rid of the lingering thoughts of abuse that will hold you back.

Release the Abuser

The relationship with an abuser is often filled with anxiety and fear. You walk on eggshells anxious that the next thing you want to do will trigger their rage, causing a fight and a further unpleasant situation. There is a tendency for this to continue long after separation from the narcissist.

While we do not doubt the fact that narcissists love losing and can be stubborn in their pursuit, realize that they are not as strong as you think. They only want you to believe they are.

With this in mind, the ability to get rid of the trauma bond will help you disarm them. You can now become established and resolute, unwavering even in the face of all their issues and drama.

Practice Mindfulness

When you stay sin an abusive relationship, you subconsciously transport yourself into a state of hyper-vigilance. You are always careful of your moves, afraid of doing anything to spook your abuser. This creates excessive stimulation of the sympathetic system, which leads to an influx of adrenaline and other stress chemicals into the blood.

The key to deactivate this is to activate the parasympathetic system. In other words, you are transitioning from fight or flight mode to rest mode. This comes from various methods such as deep breathing, mindfulness, or any activity that relaxes and eases your anxiety.

All in all, know that you can heal and break free from the shackles of an abusive relationship. Your effort to heal and recover yourself can be the ticket to a whole, integrated, and complete human being. You can improve!

Narcissism Among Friends

Friendship is a beautiful gift. You choose those that surround you, and these friends help make the world seem a little brighter and life worth living. Friends are there to catch us when we fall, and the people we are close to receive the investment of our trust and emotions. This bond can be overlooked by many, taking it for granted.

However, there are some instances where disturbing patterns, pain, and an unhealthy attachment seem to characterize the friendship. Some people are trapped in a narcissistic friendship without any idea of what that means, just that they are unhappy. Believing in someone's goodness is a basic premise of humanity. You hang on for the ride, longing for the friend you once knew to come back. Unfortunately, there are times when things can never go back.

Holding on too long can open you up to narcissistic abuse. Due to the attachment, our narcissist friend finds it easy to prey and impose on us. They see us as an extension of themselves, and nothing we ever do is good or acceptable. Worst of all, you never seem to agree on anything as your narcissist friend believes their opinions are more important, and right.

Rather than enjoying the benefit that comes from having a friend, the benefits of the relationship are one-sided. You are there to meet their needs and soothe their ego. Saying sorry is not in their dictionary, and they will never accept that they have done anything wrong. Holding on to this friendship for long starts taking its toll. By desperately trying to fix a broken friendship, we drown. Our self-worth, self-esteem and self-confidence will suffer for it. The relationship becomes draining and you are exhausted, trying to salvage it.

Narcissism is real and plagues every facet of human relationships. Even though it is a lot to take in, many people find themselves in this kind of relationship. It is disappointing and shocking that such a thing could occur among friends, but that is the reality. If you have found yourself in this kind of relationship, here are some tips to keep your sanity intact:

Be Good to Yourself: you do not need another person to complete you. Any friend that takes advantage of you should be cut out of your life. Realize that friendship does not add value to you and is not worth the time.

Free Yourself: while there is nothing wrong with trying to help your friend, know when to draw the line. This might be difficult because letting go of a friend isn't always easy. But what friendship is worth the exhaustion?

<u>Know What You Will Tolerate</u>: narcissists, even in friendship, sees everyone as less than themselves. In their world, they are superior, so they expect to be treated like it. They also operate with the mindset that they can treat everyone like trash and a nobody. Know your self-worth and what you will not tolerate from your friend. Know when to draw the line.

<u>Know When to Get Help</u>: being in a narcissistic relationship is complicated and draining. It takes its toll on almost all areas of life. There are times you might need to seek outside help in order to recover from the anguish of dealing with a narcissist. There are support groups, and therapy can be of help.

<u>Knowing when to walk away</u> from a friend or relationship takes courage. It can be a lot to process, which hurts. However, you need to protect yourself from a friendship that drains the life out of you.

Workplace Narcissism

Narcissists are peculiar people, and they are easy to spot from an outsider's perspective. They occur in every facet of human interactions, including the workplace. They are typically obnoxious, overly outspoken and can make everyone around them uncomfortable. Using various manipulation techniques like mind control, they find it easy to get people entangled in their webs. As master manipulators, they can put up a front to get on the good side of people. They are charismatic, the life of the party, risk-takers, and they know how to get others to do things for them. This makes it easy for them to rise to a leadership position.

With narcissists, all that glitters is not gold. You need to know how to protect yourself from all their mind games and manipulations. We have the following tips to protect yourself from the narcissist

How to Spot a Narcissist

This is perhaps the most important part of surviving narcissism in the workplace. You need to keep yourself updated on the signs of a narcissist so you will not be caught in their traps. Narcissists are skilled at blending in to get what they want, and developing an ability to see past their veil will help. They might come off as friendly and charismatic at first. But as we have learned, they love making friends with people they can easily take advantage of.

They believe everything they do is under the radar so calling a narcissist out on their behavior might end up backfiring. They like to employ tactics like guilt, gaslighting, and criticism to create any type of chaos in their power, even in professional settings such as the workplace. Watch out for this.

Get Your Facts Right

If the narcissist your boss, confrontation might not be the best tactic. They are not against using dark tactics to confuse and disorient you, creating an unpleasant work situation and eventually getting rid of any threats.

Letting things go is not in their nature. With this in mind, you need to be smarter in your dealings with thing. Keep tabs on everything, all you observe, what they do and say. This will go a long way in protecting you and making a case for your arguments when the time comes.

Guard Your Weaknesses

Empaths and narcissists make for a toxic relationship because narcissists see the caring and nurturing nature of the empaths as a weakness. They see these as a loophole to get attached and entangled with them. If the empath knows their forgiving nature could get them into trouble, it's a good plan to keep this fact hidden.

In other words, a narcissist will draw near you if they feel there is something they can take advantage of. This calls for knowing yourself and the attributes that make you vulnerable. If you trust people easily, have trouble saying no and do things for people freely, the narcissist might explore these traits and use them to their advantage.

Avoid Taking Things Personally

In the world of narcissists, they are the most important person. They do not care about who gets hurt and who they victimize with their games. This is just how they are wired, and it is not your fault. It boils down to their need to put others down to feel better. With this in mind, do not feel sad or bitter if they make derogatory comments or try to belittle you. It's just their insecurity showing.

Throughout the book, we have made sure not to recommend confrontation with this type of personality as it can only end in more problems. You might not win if you call them out. Stroking their ego, while being a step ahead of them, is a good way to protect yourself. Keep these points in mind and know how to play your cards right.

Chapter 7
Helping a Narcissist Recover

Y ou might wonder why we are talking about how you can help someone with narcissism when we have spent so long telling you that you can't fix them. That isn't the point. We're not suggesting that you can wave a magic wand and fix this person, allowing them to have meaningful and lasting relationships and friendships. We're suggesting that there are ways you can at least help someone, and maybe encourage them seek help.

Know right now that it might not work; narcissists are by their very nature very stubborn and are not going to accept help if they don't deem it to be strictly necessary. By suggesting that they may have a problem and need help, you are (in their eyes) attacking their very personality and self, and that will not be taken lightly.

Narcissists aren't always 100% narcissistic; you might have someone who only has narcissism when certain events trigger it, e.g. when they're rejected or go through a hard time, and as a result, their personality disorder comes to the fore. On the other hand, you might be dealing with someone who is narcissistic all the time, but not to a huge degree. These are the people you may be able to help, but for anyone who is 100%

severe and toxic in terms of narcissism, don't even bother trying. These people will not take your suggestion well, and the only way that these types of narcissistic will ever receive help is when they take everything a step too far.

So, in what ways can you actually attempt to help a narcissist? There are very few ways, but you can try and encourage them to seek help by subtle moves. Again, this depends on the type of narcissism. You should also be very prepared for rejection, but know that at least you tried. From there, you can figure out your own options and decide what your own plan of action is going to be. Remember, you can't change someone else without their will; you can only control yourself.

There are three main ways you can attempt to help someone close to you who is clearly in the grips of NPD.

Do Not Allow Them to Manipulate You

This particular step is for you mainly, but it does help them indirectly. By refusing to let them manipulate you, and by allowing their gaslighting attempts to backfire, you're actually making them sit up and take notice. They will see that you are stronger, and they will wonder why. They will not want you to leave, as they need you around, even though their behavior probably shows otherwise.

In some ways, dealing with a narcissist is like dealing with a child.

If you tell them they can't have something, but then give in, they'll simply continue that level of behavior because they know you'll give in at some point. Narcissists will do the same thing, which is why it is so important that if you say you're going to walk out of the room when they belittle you, you actually do it. Do not apologize for something that isn't your fault and do not bow down to their demands. This will take practice, and it will be hard, but by looking after yourself and your own needs first, you will find the strength to do it.

By ensuring that their tactics backfire, you're taking away a huge amount of their power. This could go one of two ways : they could turn angry and simply lash out at your attempts, or they could possibly start to soften. It depends on the level of narcissism they are afflicted with. Of course, if they lash out, cut your losses and walk away. You've tried, and there's nothing more you can do.

Wait Until They are Calm, and Have a Discussion

If you've tried step one and it didn't go badly, e.g. they softened a little, then perhaps this second step will help. Remember that in order for someone to seek help, it has to be their decision. It's no good forcing someone to see a doctor if they don't believe anything is wrong with them. Think about an alcoholic, for instance. You can't force this person to admit they need help. The first step towards recovery is knowing there is a problem in the first place.

The types of treatment for NPD all hinge on a total commitment to the treatment at hand. If someone doesn't really believe they need help, the treatment isn't going to work at all. So, the point of this step is to simply sow a seed in their mind and help them explore the possibilities.

Wait until they are calm to sit down and have a conversation. Be soft and don't be forceful. Talk to them, not at them, and make sure that you keep your emotions on an even keel. Tell them that you feel like they're treating you in an unfair way and give examples to back up your words. Tell them that you know they don't mean to treat you this way and they are a good person. If they remain calm, you may be able to make progress. If they simply throw a narcissistic tantrum and turn it around, again, you can't do anymore.

Find some literature on NPD and leave it on the table. Tell them that you've found this information and perhaps they might like to read it. Suggest you read it together, or they can read it on their own, and you'll be by their side whatever they decide.

Remember, it's not 100% guaranteed that this step will work, but it's worth a try if you want to know you did all you could before you decide to walk away. It's also important that by some stroke of luck, they agree to perhaps talk about things over with a health professional, and they recognize there might be something not quite right. Then you remain supportive and on their side at all times. Remember that deep down, a narcissistic is lacking in confidence and needs constant reassurance. The fact that you've suggested there might be something wrong could go either way, but by being calm and supportive - being on their side at all times - you may be able to guide them through it and toward professional help.

Issue an Ultimatum

This is the final method to try, and it's not one you should attempt as the first port of call. This is not likely to go well, but there is a chance. By issuing an ultimatum, you're basically saying, "look, I do not want to be treated in this way, but I know it's now what you really mean to do deep down. I'm giving you one chance to sort this out, and I will be by your side all the way. If you refuse, and if you continue to act in this way, I will leave for good."

You have to go through with your ultimatum and do not attempt to go back on it. Be strong and see it through, whatever way it goes. The point of this, however, is not to shout and lecture, it's a firm statement of intent. If you add emotions and hysterics, they are not going to take you seriously.

These are the only ways you can attempt to help someone with NPD, without actually being a health professional. Even if you were a health professional, the person would need to be willing to seek help and make a commitment to really putting in the effort to change. Treatment for NPD is quite intensive and requires a lot of deep thinking and behavioral change. It requires a strong will to make it work, so you can see why someone being forced to seek help is not going to have a good outcome.

The Importance of Knowing You Cannot "Save" Anyone

We've said this once, and we need to say it again. You cannot "save" a person with NPD, and you cannot fix them. This intention can only come from themselves. It's sad to walk away from someone who has a condition and doesn't actually "mean" to act in a certain way, but at the same time, you can't wave a magic wand and make it all go away again either.

The only thing you can do is focus on yourself and go with what you feel is right. You know in your gut that you deserve happiness and if your partner/friend or whoever this person is to you is not going to give you that, the only thing you can do for yourself is walk away. If you are in a relationship with this person, what would happen if children come into the equation? Would you want them to be born into a relationship with a large narcissistic element? That is certainly something to think about.

Make sure you have this fact in your mind before you attempt to help someone with NPD and before you make a decision to walk away. By knowing that in a solid and firm manner, you won't have regrets about your final actions.

Highly narcissistic people are usually unaware that they are so as they live very often in a state of denial and are unlikely to attempt to improve or work on themselves.

The Future for a Narcissist Who Refuses Help

It doesn't paint a great picture if the person isn't willing to seek help. In that case, it's far more likely that the narcissist will end up jumping from destructive relationship to destructive relationship, and if they do end up in a long-term union, it's unlikely that their partner will be truly happy and fulfilled. That person is far more likely to be simply "putting up" with the narcissism.

If a narcissist ends up in a relationship that yields children, the sad truth is that their children are quite likely to develop narcissistic tendencies as a result during their early years. While there isn't a certain answer to what causes NPD, there a definite suggestion that childhood experiences create a firm link to the personality in their adolescent and then adult years.

Narcissists also have the habit of becoming quite bitter over time. This is partly because people have come into their lives and left them, and they can't see why. Of course, they will project the blame onto the other person and don't see their role in them leaving. Many narcissistic traits, therefore, worsen with age, as more experiences are racked up throughout life.

As you can see, it's quite a bleak picture we're painting. and that is the sad truth about life as a narcissist. People can only stand being treated a certain way for so long before they eventually pluck up the courage to leave. While some never get to that point, these relationships are likely to be empty and lacking in true love and respect. For these reasons, the biggest price a narcissist pays for their actions over time is loneliness and a lack of a truly meaningful relationships in the end. For a narcissistic, however, the most loving and deep relationship they have is with themselves.

Chapter 8
The Narcissist and Empathy

When it's Time to Leave

At this point, your partner must be willing to at least try to make some changes in their behavior to improve their own mental health and the relationship. If your partner is willing to do some of the work, then your relationship can be saved. But, if you have been engaging in the activities discussed previously in this book, and your partner still does not see any problem with their behavior, there isn't much hope for an improvement.

Unfortunately, as much as we want to believe that we can change another person, we cannot always do so. You can change the dynamics on your end, which can improve the relationship for you, but in order for your partner to truly overcome their narcissistic traits, they have to put in some effort on their own. This chapter will outline some of the things that your partner can do to improve their narcissistic tendencies. These techniques are the last step to turn a narcissist into a loving and attentive partner.

Identify the Maladaptive Behaviors that Need to be Changed

What types of behaviors does your partner see as maladaptive or problematic? This could come from a list that you make or your partner understands to be true, or a combination of both. Once your partner acknowledges the inappropriate behaviors, he or she can begin to attack and alter them head on.

Once you both know and understand the types of behaviors to work on, you can set up a positive and negative reinforcement system. Basically, if your partner does something positive to change their behavior, they should be rewarded somehow, and if they engage in one of the behaviors you are trying to get rid of, a form of negative reinforcement (often called punishment) should be used like the "No Contact" principle. It works when, for instance, your partner gets abusive, and you distance yourself from him or her to protect yourself and cool things off. Your partner will eventually realize his or her mistake and will ask you to deal with the problem.

The punishments and rewards should be worked out between you both, and your partner has to be willing to commit to them. Many studies have shown that positive reinforcement works better than negative long term, so it makes sense to reward all small behaviors. If these rewards involve both of you, it could be a great way to strengthen your bond.

Practice Service to Others

People can learn to care for others. They have to choose to put the needs of another person before their own needs. If your narcissistic partner is willing to try this, it will be the first step to a more loving partnership. To do so, your partner should put aside one of their needs and do something for you no matter how simple or small. Whether it means running an errand that you usually do, making dinner, or taking care of one small thing so you don't have to, ask your partner to do something just for you. Start with something small, and over time, your partner will develop the ability to do more and more.

If your partner is willing to do these things for you, it is a good sign that they are willing to change. Talking about each other's needs and deciding the boundaries on both sides of the relationship is important. If your partner is amenable to do things for you, you, yourself, should be ready to do things for them as well, especially with regard to their mental health and stability. As discussed earlier, you have the right to say no to unreasonable demands, but, in a loving relationship, you have to give as well. But it must be reasonable.

Your partner will learn that providing a service to others will benefit both of you, and your partner will experience personal joy from seeing you happy, but it takes practice. Service to others is important to develop empathy for another person, which is the next step in the process.

Practice Empathy

Simply defined, empathy is the ability to put yourself in another person's place. By imagining how another person feels, you can relate to them better. The narcissist needs to do this, and it is a skill that takes practice. You can facilitate this by explaining to your partner how you feel when they do a certain thing. As they begin to understand this, they will be better able to put themselves in the position of another. Once your partner can understand how another person feels, they will be more likely to help them.

Don't Take Life so Seriously

To someone with narcissism, not getting their way seems like a life and death situation. But examining what happens if the narcissist doesn't get their way makes it easier to understand that horrible things will most likely not happen. The narcissist needs to remind themselves that they are not perfect, and they do not have to be. They need to look for the humor in little things. As soon as they learn not to take life so seriously, humor can be found. And tomorrow, it probably won't even be that important.

Once your partner realizes that even though yesterday seemed like a life and death situation, it's not the same as the present situation, and it will become easier to laugh at their own mistakes and move forward in a more loving way. When everything is no longer about them and they face the fact that they cannot get everything they want and learn that it is not a crisis, things will get easier. They will learn to let go of things and move on more easily. Your partner will learn that they do not have to have control of everything and that life will not fall apart.

Practice Self-Compassion

If your narcissist is the grandiose type, it is all the more important to practice self-compassion rather than develop self-esteem. Your narcissistic partner already has plenty of confidence, and this is what makes them think they are entitled to everything they want and desire. Instead, fostering self-compassion will help promote tenderness for other people. And, in the end, what will cause your partner to change their behavior is understanding that everyone deserves love and respect. It starts with loving and respecting themselves.

To foster self-compassion, consider the three steps: developing self-kindness, understanding our common humanity, and practicing mindfulness.

Self-kindness is the simple idea that we should not beat ourselves up when something goes wrong. It means that when we talk to ourselves in our mind, it should be kind, rather than harsh. If you or your partner makes a mistake, what thoughts go through your mind? Do you berate yourself or do you try to comfort yourself? Most narcissists will berate themselves and then lash out to try and make they feel better. Instead of lashing out at themselves, they should practice saying kind things in their mind. Remind yourself that everyone makes mistakes and it's okay not to be perfect because no one is. Say nice things to yourself.

Second, realizing that everyone faces the same struggles will help to connect to that common bond we call humanity. Everyone has imperfections. Everyone feels insecure at times, and everyone has problems. When you practice self-compassion, you put yourself on the same level with everyone else around you. This is a necessary step for the narcissist. When they are able to do this, they can stop treating everyone else as if they are only meant to serve their needs. They will realize that they are part of a greater whole, not above it. This will make it easier for them to change their behaviors. This is a key realization to turn a narcissist into a loving human being: that everyone comes from the same place and has issues from various roots. No one's problems or ideas are more important than another's.

Lastly, the narcissist must learn to practice mindfulness which means keeping their thoughts in the present moment. It also means acknowledging their feelings as they happen and thus dealing immediately with them. Suppressing what one thinks and feels causes emotional outbursts later. By dealing with them in the present moment, the narcissist will be less likely to act out in negative ways.

By working through these steps, the narcissist can be turned into a thoughtful and loving person. Self-compassion, when practiced regularly, will naturally transform into compassion for the world around them. It will need much effort and will take time. Doing these things is not an easy, but the benefits for both the narcissist, and you, as the partner, will be immensely gratifying.

Understanding Gas Lighting

Gas lighting comes from the movie of the same name that was released in 1944. It refers to a manipulation tactic some people use, especially the narcissist, to try and cause doubt in the minds of their victims. The way a person gaslights depends on the situation, but the main objective remains the same. They want to reinvent past events to make sure their errors or mistakes stay hidden.

In the example above, Margaret clearly remembers that her mother spanked her and her siblings. This was verified by the conversation she had with her brother, so she knew she hadn't made it up. When her mother noticed how good her granddaughter acted, she knew that Margaret's parenting was working, which showed her choice of spanking wasn't the best discipline method.

With this in mind, Margaret's mother wanted to create distance between her and that discipline practice since it has become seen as harmful, ineffective, and unnecessary. She chose to claim she never did it, despite the fact Margaret and her brother remember having to face it as children.

With this example, the gas lighting seems relatively harmless and Margaret could just brush it off. But with narcissistic gas lighting, it becomes extreme, and it can create serious doubt and even cause their victim to start questioning their sanity. This is only one tactic that a narcissist will use to protect their image, not just how they appear in the present, but in the past as well. They have to make sure that they appear correct in every part of their life, so they strive to stay away from being branded for little mistakes even if they took place decades ago. Gas lighting allows them to sweep these mistakes under the rug while also hurting a person's sanity, which to them, means nothing.

Smear Tactic

If you start to notice that people distance themselves from you once you get out of the clutches of the narcissist, they have probably started a smear campaign. While politics typically holds the most popular smear campaigns, narcissists will sometimes use these same strategies. Once you cut ties with a narcissist, they have realized something: you know who they truly are. This means that if you were to start exposing the narcissist for whom they really are, which likely isn't even a part of your plan, then they are going to have to be carefully because their façade may start to crumble. This isn't something that they want to face.

What is a narcissist to do? They will use smear campaigns to stay a step ahead of the game. They use the information they have about you and the relationship you had. They will make sure to talk with mutual friends before you do to clarify the reasons why you two are no longer speaking. This will likely involve tweaking some information to make you out to be the bad guy.

It's important to note that a narcissist is not going to settle for just mentioning a couple of nasty things. They are looking to completely destroy your reputation and credibility. This ensures that you will have a very hard time convincing your friends what you really experienced. You will come off as unreliable, and they keep the friends and their reputation.

If the narcissist chooses to do a smear campaign, it can leave you without anyone to turn to. Some gossip and rumors can be so bad that it harms your job and other relationships. Keep in mind that they never really cared about you to begin with, so don't be surprised if they become somebody unrecognizable and start sharing absolute lies about you and the things you have done.

Abuse by Surrogate

The one thing that a narcissist never runs out of is people. People gravitate towards them for the same reason you did. Unfortunately, if somebody chooses to cross a narcissist, they will find themselves dealing with attacks from the rest of their posse.

This is something that you could refer to as abuse by surrogate, and it will start the moment you upset them. Their need to discourage and shame will hit full force, and they are going to make sure that you feel their unhappiness for what you have done to them. They will also take things a step further and hit where it hurts. This is where other people will step in.

Narcissists, as discussed above, will start to talk to other people in their circle about you. They will convince them that you are the one at fault, and you must be taught a lesson. The interesting thing is that they won't actually say those exact words. It looks more like brainwashing when making other people believe certain lies and encouraging them to act on certain ideas without instruction.

Here's an example: Damito is the middle child. Her sisters are A+ students and they bring home impeccable report cards and get a lot of praise from their teachers. Damito is just an average student. While she may not get the grades her siblings do, she does come home with decent grades. She is by no means failing. One day, though, she fails an exam and her mother loses her mind. She reprimands her, says she's lazy and that she is worried about her future. She says that her performance isn't going to get her anywhere in life, and it upsets her to say that Damito isn't going to achieve what her sisters will.

Damito is sent to her room after being reprimanded in front of the family at dinner. She cries and sulks in her room for the rest of the night. Meanwhile, her sisters are still at the dinner table, and her mother continues to complain. She praises Damito's sisters. The great grades give meaning to the long hours she spends at work to afford their schooling. The children feel happy and loved by their mother's words, and they thank her for all of the effort she has put in to make sure that they can get the best education.

While they are talking, she calls Damito ungrateful, saying she doesn't deserve to get the same opportunities as her sisters because she doesn't appreciate what her mother does. She goes on to tell them that they shouldn't associate with people like Damito because they can be bad influences and cause them to lose sight of the things that are important. Before their conversation comes to an end, she says that she still has to work hard and hopes for the best, even if some of them don't appreciate what she does. The end their conversation and the kids go to bed.

The following day, Damito gets up and heads to the kitchen for breakfast to find that all of the food has been eaten. "You got up late, so you don't get food," her older sister tells her rudely. During the day Damito is showered with the same harsh and negative energy from her sisters who seem to be avoiding her.

This makes her feel ashamed and alone. This causes her to approach her mother and apologize for being ungrateful for all of the work she has done. Her mother "accepts" her daughter's apology, but she stays cold towards her daughter in the next few days, which her sisters mimic. Can you see the problem in this scenario?

First, it's important to see the reason for the aggravation. What did Damito do to get this kind of treatment from her mother and then her sisters? A single failed test. For the majority of us, one bad grade isn't a reason to get this upset. In fact, most parents would let this slide with saying more than, "do better next time."

However, since Damito's mother is a narcissist, she views any type of failure as completely unacceptable. Her children are an extension of her, so if they have any shortcomings, it is completely unforgivable because if reflects badly on her. She made a point of reprimanding Damito in front of her sisters. This shows her anger and imparts shame because everybody else gets to hear and see her receiving this punishment.

Next, once Damito leaves, and her mother continues to talk with her sisters. She starts out by praising them, telling them how proud she is of them being top students. Of course, it's easy to infer that they only perform well because of the pressure from their mother and not because they actually want to do well. By talking to Damito's sisters, she can trick them into feeling the same animosity towards Damito, who didn't even do anything malicious to anybody in the family.

Her sisters and her mother don't have a real reason to be upset with her because the grade she gets doesn't affect any of them. However, since her mother used the tactic of divide and conquer, they feel connected to her and thus become aligned by mimicking how she feels. What happens next? They unknowingly emotionally abuse Damito by giving her the cold shoulder. They distance themselves and treat her like a pariah. This causes Damito to feel the brunt of her "mistake" and she has no choice but to apologize, even though she shouldn't have to.

Abuse by surrogate can be hard to handle because it causes the victim to feel isolated. They start questioning themselves and may even begin to believe their abuser had a good reason to treat them so badly. What's more, they feel the added pressure from the "mob" which complicates their internal battle. If everybody is mad at me, then I must have done something wrong.

What is important to remember here is that just because several people believe something doesn't make it true. When you are at the brunt end of abuse by surrogate, it can cause you to start questioning your validity and integrity, but you stay strong and decide to believe that the truth will help you to be less affected by their abuse and disapproval.

Dealing with Emotional Abuse

If you or your partner find these steps quite difficult, it can be useful to seek professional help. A therapist or counselor can be an impartial guide in following these steps and can provide essential insight that you both missed. They can make sure that the two of you are not seeking to hurt each other, even unintentionally. Although not necessary, a therapist can be a valuable asset in the quest of turning your narcissist partner into an unselfish, loving partner.

It is my sincere hope that you and your partner are both willing to put the work necessary into your relationship to improve it. By following the techniques laid out in this book, you will have the person you love turn into a thoughtful, unselfish partner. But they, too, have to be willing to do the work. Remember, you cannot force someone to change. You can change how you act, but if your partner is not willing to engage in the work laid out in this chapter, there is only so much you can do to improve your relationship. But, working together, you and your partner can accomplish miraculous things. You can get the loving partner you want while and he or she learns to deal with life and relationships more effectively.

Chapter 9
Healing from Narcissistic Abuse

T o the people reading this who have survived narcissistic abuse, good for you. Now it is time for the healing to begin. The good news is that there are many approaches you can take to get your life back in order. In applying the various healing techniques, be sure to give yourself time. The abuse did not occur overnight, and neither will your reparations. With these thoughts in mind, here are the recommended healing techniques to revitalize your life after narcissistic abuse.

Meditation

Meditation is a great way to center yourself through active body movement and deep breathing. Healing narcissist abuse brings victims face to face with their source of fear. The memories and images of past abuse that may have been buried will likely be brought to light once you quiet your mind. The intention of this practice is to help you embrace your past experiences, good or bad, while disarming the traumatic effect the bad thoughts have had on you.

Studies have established that meditation can help combat symptoms of PTSD (Cohut, 2019). Meditation reduces the stress hormones by soothing our sympathetic nervous system, which triggers the fight or flight hormones. We have included the following tips to help with peaceful meditation specifically dealing with trauma.

Find a Safe Place to Meditate

After leaving the abuser and ending the toxic relationship, there is a tendency to have flashbacks that trigger panic attacks. The presence of your abuser matters as it reinforces the attacks.

For meditation to be effective, you must feel safe. This feeling of peace must sink into your subconscious so that you relax and feel unencumbered. Find a quiet spot where you are alone, lay out a mat, maybe light some candles. Put on meditation music or "ohm" in a low tone to keep distractions at bay. Breathe, as this is the beginning of healing.

Find Other Ways to Meditate

There are many approaches to mindfulness. In fact, should you develop panic attack or anxiety, doing something, anything, to keep yourself distracted can help. It can be while washing the dishes. With every stroke of the sponge, you can drift into a state of mindfulness. It could be while mowing the lawn, brushing your teeth, etc. All you are to do is focus your thoughts on the task at hand. With this, you are not actively attempting to meditate but to complete your chores.

Be a Witness to Your Flashbacks

It is common for victims of abuse to have physical reactions to any thoughts of their abuse or abuser. With meditation, you can witness your thoughts in a controlled setting rather than reacting to them. While reliving the memories of your abuse, it does not have to paralyze you as it did before. With meditation, you can be a gentle observer of the memories of your abuse. This way, you can strengthen your control which will lead to a significant improvement over time.

Group Therapy for Healing

Group therapy involves the coming together of people in similar situations who have experienced narcissistic abuse. These share their struggles and how they were overcome. This allows victims to come to terms with the fact that they are not alone. Group therapy exposes victims to various approaches through which they can heal. Group therapy offers patience, courage, and strength to heal, recover, and eventually get your mental health in order. It can help tap into the inner strength needed to live a healthy and satisfying life.

A Typical Group Therapy Session

Group therapy is handled by a trained therapist and the sessions consist of six to twelve members all sharing their stories. The idea is for people with similar characteristics (in this case, victims of a narcissist's abuse) to voice their concerns, experiences, and coping strategies in a safe environment. Group therapy works best in combination with meditation and other forms of therapy.

The idea of sharing your nightmares in a room full of strangers might be scary, but it has a wide range of benefits. With the diversity that exists within a group, the victims of narcissistic abuse can develop new and healthy strategies. Hearing others share their tale of abuse can do a lot for your journey.

Types of Group Therapy

Most group therapy occurs in two forms: process-oriented group therapy and psycho-educational group therapy. In the process-oriented group experience, the therapist does not take a major role. They only act as a moderator and encourage members to share. This creates a sense of belonging in each member and a feeling that they are in charge of the session. This is the type of group therapy that best helps victims of narcissistic abuse.

The psycho-educational group experience, on the other hand, puts the therapist in charge. He teaches members healthy and scientifically-tested coping skills to solve various life problems. The therapist is the center of attention here as they play the role of teacher.

Cognitive Behavioral Therapy for Narcissistic Abuse Recovery

Over the years, CBT has proven to be pretty effective in helping trauma victims. The aim is to bring improvement by systematically changing patterns of thoughts, feelings, and behaviors. CBT revolves around the fact that the three are connected and an improvement in one can trigger an improvement in another.

With CBT, patients can learn:

- Helpful coping mechanisms for stress and how to handle trauma
- To interact with their trauma in a new way that does not trigger a negative reaction
- How to develop an objective understanding of their relationship with the narcissist to help revive their sense of control and also develop healthy coping skills.

The therapist helps victims to reconsider their thinking patterns to detect unhelpful patterns. These are the patterns that might have occurred due to continuous exposure to the abuse. For instance, victims might think they are bad people for attracting a narcissist. Unbeknownst to them, narcissists do not take an interest in weak or insignificant people. They prefer to go for strong and powerful people who can soothe their egos, people they can exploit. Victims, however, do not know this. With this therapy, victims begin to see themselves in a new light. The aim is to help bring the traumatic experience to a new light. This way, they get a new perspective about the incidence as well as their ability to cope.

Many times, victims of narcissistic abuse avoid and suppress memories of the abuse or anything that triggers their time with the abuser. CBT can help reduce this by assisting patients in embracing the occurrence in a healthy way. This involves a planned and controlled exposure in a way and at a pace that the patient is comfortable with. This bring control and confidence, rather than resorting to avoidance behaviors.

Yoga for Narcissistic Abuse Healing

Over the years, yoga has grown in popularity as a means of connecting the mind and body. As a mindfulness exercise that uses various breathing and relaxation techniques combined with physical movement, yoga has proven to successfully treat mental health issues as well as trauma from past occurrences.

Continuous exposure to stress and potentially life-threatening situations reconfigures the body into fight-or-flight mode. Even though this is the body's way of saving us from danger, excessive stress raises the cortisol level that we know triggers mental health problems.

Yoga has a soothing effect on all levels of stress in the body. It can calm the body and transport it to a state of tranquility. A common factor with victims of trauma is the inability to adequately process and heal from their experiences. This is why traditional therapy alone is not very helpful.

Introducing Trauma-Sensitive Yoga

Trauma-based yoga stands out in that it directs the body awareness of the present moment to take care of any symptoms arising from abuse or trauma. This emphasizes the internal experiences of the victim who is intending to get in touch with their body at the present moment.

These helpful feelings could be anything from how the cloth hugs their body to the movement of air through their lungs. The aim is exposing how they can take action about their experience. With this yoga practice, students can learn to get in touch with their bodies and minds.

Yoga, in combination with psychotherapy, can help reduce the after effects of trauma and narcissistic abuse while reinforcing positive emotions such as acceptance, compassion, and empowerment.

Self-Hypnosis for Healing

Hypnosis is a way to reach memories that are out of one's consciousness. Self-hypnosis tries to provide a positive restructuring to dissociated traumatic memories. In other words, with self-hypnosis, victims can face their fears and the traumatic time spent with the narcissist. Rather than being hindered by the memory, patients embrace these memories in a new dimension. This is done with the aim of re-moralizing memories like self-protection and at times, pity for the abuser.

With this, victims can access the traumatic memory in a controlled way while viewing them from a broader perspective. There are many forms of self-hypnosis, but we will run through the eye fixation self-hypnosis method in this book. Be sure you are in a quiet room without distractions. Get into a comfortable position and make sure you are well seated without crossing your legs and feet. Your clothes should not be too tight, and we suggest no shoes.

Look up and take a deep breath. Pick a point on the ceiling and direct your gaze, without straining your neck. With your gaze fixed in this position, breathing in deeply, pause, and exhale. Repeat this for sometimes and relax. Close your eyes and feel every tension in your body drift out. Allow Your Body to Relax. Let go of all tension in your body and sit in a relaxed position. Countdown from five and let your body relax deeper with every count. Direct your attention to your breath, note the rising and falling of your chest. The key is not in trying to relax your body. Rather, it is in allowing your body to relax.

Bring Back Your Consciousness

Count from one to five and open your eyes. Open your eyes at the count of five, stretch your arms and legs

You might not feel as calm as you would want. The key is growing with practice as there is a learning curve.

Using EMDR to Heal Narcissistic Abuse

With Eye Movement Desensitization and Reprocessing (EMDR), victims can unlock past hurtful experiences. It is not a traditional therapy and works best over a few sessions. It has healing effects on the thoughts, feelings, and memories of the past, and in this case, narcissistic abuse.

EMDR is an intense form of therapy in that it seeks to unlock painful memories, associated with the abuser. It is a psychotherapy that helps people heal and recover from the emotional distress of a traumatic event.

Humans generally have either the left or right brain hemisphere dominant. However, EMDR with bilateral stimulation helps activate both sides. Since they both work at the same speed and capacity, there is rapid processing. This reconfiguration makes it easy to identify trauma by highlighting the affected area. Rather than the trauma being stuck, it gets processed in a healthy manner.

Many victims of abuse, specifically narcissistic abuse, react to the memory of the trauma like it just happened. Part of the aim of EMDR is to curtail this. For instance, you remember how your abusive partner yells at you. Nothing you did was good enough which made you sad and angry. The difference now is that even though you remember every detail; you do not feel the anger.

This is what EMDR is trying to achieve. It helps reprocess the memory such that even if you remember how hurtful the experience of the abuse was, you no longer feel the physical manifestation. Not only do you have a renewed approach to these memories, but you also have to let go of the hatred and resentment you had for your partner.

Chapter 10
Dating After Leaving a Narcissist

G etting back control of your life after years of abuse might seem like a difficult thing to do. But with the right guidance and using the right tools, you can effectively regain your control and find happiness again.

Get the Negativity Out of Your System

Like it or not, there is a whole lot of negativity within your system by the time you are parting with a narcissist. This toxicity accumulated as you tried to appease them and in trying to make the relationship work. You tried to understand the narcissist as they took advantage of you more and more. It is now time to let go of all that darkness and allow space for your life to take shape again.

Some of the things you can do to get this negativity out include journaling or sharing your story with a friend, or even engaging a therapist. Talking out the story is so helpful, especially when it is with a listening partner since it helps in organizing your confused thoughts into place. Also, it helps to empower you since you can finally be honest with yourself. You can engage in mind and body exercises such as yoga or dancing that help to discard the toxicity and clears your mind to accommodate positivity.

Compile a List of the Controlling Incidents you Have Experienced

Although this might seem trivial, compiling the experiences of control and abuse helps you realize what you have been through and appreciate your growth - the fact that you will not allow yourself to be in such a situation again. Such remembrance gives you pride in your bravery in leaving and looking forward to a more rewarding life. You appreciate that you can now live as a free person and cannot allow yourself to fall back in the abusive relationship.

Practice Listening to Your Inner Self

Your inner voice is the best tool you will ever have in dealing with any situation. It shows you how best you can do things and it never lies. Even amid great pain and desperation, your inner voice will show you how to find your way out. The major reason why the narcissist was able to manipulate you was that they worked on the external stimulants of your brain, which in turn messed your internal stimulants as argued by Morf, Horvath and Torchetti (2011). They were fulfilling their selfish motives by controlling how your brain responds to things. However, listening to your inner voice will help you review a situation and you can learn when to move ahead, hold back, or reject the things being said to you. It will guide you in your newly acquired life, one in which you are free. Now you understand yourself much better and will never fall for a toxic person again.

Organizing Time and Space

It is good to have a clean and organized space since this allows you enough time to absorb everything that comes your way. When your space is full of clutter, you feel overwhelmed because it registers in your mind that you have a lot to do. Decluttering allows you to organize your space and keep only the things that matter to you. You will find that your brain will respond positively to living in an ordered place. You will feel more settled and you are energized to face every new day. Also, clutter obscures your mind and your thinking. You can establish a good daily routine where your most significant tasks are allocated to the time of the day you tend to be most active.

Connect with Family and Friends

As noted, narcissists usually isolate their victims from their loved ones and friends. They no longer understand you, and they may even think that you hate them. They have judged you countless times because your attitude towards them has changed. Some of them could have tried to tell you that you are not okay in your relationship, but you have always denied their sentiments in an attempt to defend your narcissist partner, who had already conditioned you to support them against all forms of attack. Since you have been dependent on the narcissist for all your social contact needs, you find it difficult to associate with people. The truth is, however, that your loved ones are always eager to reconnect and spend time with you.

Be Patient: Take Your Time

The worst mistake you can commit is to judge yourself and think you are not making fast progress regarding getting out of the pit and forgetting your narcissist. You should not be hard on yourself. Instead, understand that healing takes time to be effective. Also, everyone needs different amounts of time to get over something. Based on the depth of your abuse or length of the toxic relationship, you might need more or less time to heal.

There is no time limit on healing. Remember, your abuser has already separated you from your most precious people and hobbies. They conditioned you into feeling lost and lonely without them. Therefore, healing might take time, and it is upon you to be kind to yourself and patient as you heal. Most importantly, do not jump right into another relationship. This will obscure your thinking and deny you time to heal.

Consequently, you will carry the burden right into the next relationship, and it will not be healthy.

Acknowledge What has Been and Forgive Yourself

You might be tempted to beat yourself up for allowing such a toxic person in your life for such a long time. However, true healing and regaining power entails accepting that you have associated yourself with a highly toxic person, who has consciously hurt you. Accept that you have been tricked and abused. Trying to please them and showing them that you understood them denied you the chance to identify the red flags. Also, they used your strengths against you: you were caring, you had a good job, you were highly organized, open to new ideas, and financially stable. You never deserved this, and it was wrong of them to abuse you.

After acknowledging this, know that it was not your fault and forgive yourself. Forgiving yourself is the most important thing you need to do right now. No matter how much time, energy, wellness, and cash you have lost, that is all in the past. You have to forgive yourself and move forward. It does not matter why you stayed for so long, but it does not matter why you were fooled. But it already happened. So, forgive yourself.

Seek to Acquire Knowledge: do Self-Inquiry

It seems so difficult to make sense of the abuse you have been through and what to do after this. For such a long time you have only learned to see the world through the perspective of your abuser. You are now confused and are wondering where to begin. Seek to be knowledgeable about emotional wellness. There are a myriad of articles and online courses you have access to that can help you.

Knowledge is power, and enhancing your power never goes out of fashion.

Shift Your Focus

Because you have been abused for a long period it is easy to find your mind moving back to these thoughts. These are aspects of trauma and cognitive dissonance and are a hindrance to proper recovery. The reason why your mind keeps on pushing you back there is that it wants to comprehend certain things and process related emotions.

You should not entertain these thoughts about the past but capitalize on the present. You may find yourself taking one step forward and two steps backward. Train your mind to be in the present and the future you have chosen to make for yourself. To boost your motivation in this endeavor, you need to resurrect your dreams - and this time let them be magnificent. Remember the dreams and things you wanted for yourself before being drawn to the narcissist; think about how bad you wanted them and boost your desire to achieve them. This is what it means to shift your focus to looking forward and changing your status from that of a victim to a hero in your life. Even though you have been through pain, after healing you may be surprised by the self-loving person - aware, whole, and integrated - you have become.

Chapter 11
Case Study and its Implications

W e will now take the case study of a patient called Diana, who visited an individual therapist. This is what was gathered from the therapist's point of view. Diana was raised by a narcissist mother who blamed her for almost everything. The mother would be aggressive to Diana; then, she would tell her poor daughter that it was her fault that her mother treated her that way. Diana grew up with low self-esteem. She became a target for a narcissist partner and fell for him. Finally, she was mistreated, abused, and left in trauma. Luckily she decided to seek help. In the therapist's room, all Diana would do was to blame herself and protect her abuser.

The therapist finally asked, what do you get from blaming yourself and protecting your abuser? What do you get out of protecting your abusive ex and blaming yourself instead?

This was a hard question for Diana, who finally said, I know I made him abuse me. I provoked him. There is something I could have done to make him treat me better. Earlier, he was very nice, and he used to make me feel confident. He always praised me and told me how special I was. I am not ready to accept that he had a personality disorder. There must be a way for me to get him back and fix things the way they were.

The therapist's view

It can be tough for Diana to heal from narcissist abuse. The reason is her history of being forced to believe that it is her mistake to be ill-treated. Her childhood was fractured; she was not appreciated. She fell quickly to the flattery of a narcissist partner. She is stuck and only wants to focus on the good part. We keep on wishing that she get back the excellent experience that first carried her away. Diana blames herself so much, thinking she would have done better if her alleged suitor had remained kind to her.

The reasons why a narcissist becomes abusive are to bring others down and keep them from outshining them. Furthermore, they do it to bring other people under their manipulations. They like being bossy. They feel fulfilled and secure when they know they can order people around them without resistance. A narcissist knows well that they cannot just control grown-up human beings as quickly, so they have well-mastered tactics to achieve it. The narcissist pretends, lies, baits, lures, destroys, and steals the sense of self from their targeted victims. They do their tricks in a much-hidden way such that the victims will not realize that they are succumbing to toxic manipulation.

Diana was taken through all the stages of therapy, and she is now reconciled with reality. The same Diana was told to write another statement of the real things that her mind tells her, but her brain does not want to believe.

What Diana wrote

It is not my fault that he was abusive. There is nothing I could have done to make him treat me better. He has a history of being offensive. He only treats women well in the beginning when he wants to seal the deal. He will eventually mistreat the other woman he is using to hurt me. Other men will find me attractive and love me sincerely .

The Fate of a Narcissist

It is very devastating to see a narcissist get away with their hurtful deeds. You have been traumatized, mistreated, abused, threatened, and deprived of your happiness, and then the narcissist abuser is basking in the sunshine, enjoying his new life to the fullest as if you had never existed. This makes you think that the order of things in the universe has no room for serving justice, even for a religious person, who finds their faith distorted and starts thinking there is no compassionate creator who watches over good people. In your mind, many unanswered questions can be tossed and turned; you are wondering why the wrong people get rewarded while the competent people get hurt and destroyed.

Let's try to answer some questions: Do narcissists enjoy the rest of their lives without karma serving them their just desert? Do they continue destroying people and getting away with it? The answer is no. No matter how long it takes, everyone ends up with what they deserve. This benevolent universe grants us divine compensation for what we have lost and immense tribulation to the abusers. We do not need to do anything to make this happen; it just happens naturally.

Getting the bigger picture of the fate of a narcissist can be the key to recovery. People often ask themselves, when is the narcissist going to pay for all the horrifying things they took me through? The truth is that they pay for it every second of their lives. You may not directly understand this, for maybe you see them succeeding in life with big cars, big houses, and new lovers who appears to outdo you while harbor your pain and loneliness, with no single penny to your name!

True happiness comes from within and not without. The most valuable riches one can possess are the riches of being your true self. This is one thing the narcissist lacks. Understanding this, you can start to connect, get passionate, and create wealth from other beings. Make sure what you do is heartfelt and sincere and whatever you attain brings peace and satisfaction. If only you release that distorted perception instilled in you by the narcissist, fulfilling success is on its way. This is opposed to the narcissist who doesn't experience their true self and has no permanent connections to anything. They may appear ambitious, for there are always fantasizing about new heights of success. But in reality, this is a perversion that costs them a lot. A narcissist does not find permanent happiness, whatever is exciting to them now will be lifeless and unworthy sooner or later.

Their need for a new supply of emotional and physical things is insatiable. Eventually, they get devastated. The universal system gives more than being to a person, and the narcissist ends up being more frustrated, and feeling more pain and emptiness than other people think. The narcissist is an accurate representation of a disconnect. They have a disconnect even with their cautiousness. They cannot experience love and any other life force. This makes it challenging to come out of their devastation. They further fall into drug abuse and other self-destruction activities.

Nevertheless, as a person who wants to heal and move on with life, it is good to focus not on where the narcissist will end up but on yourself. It is good to know that they will pay for their misdeeds. As for you, concentrate on yourself. Instead of stalking them to find out how much karma has done, focus your precocious energy on how to heal with life, get your true self back, and stand on your feet again.

A narcissist hides their true self. So, even if they are going through hell, they make people believe they are succeeding. If you base your happiness in seeing them suffer, you might not be pleased in the long run. Base your happiness on yourself, who you are, who you are becoming, and the good things that are on their way.

Narcissists' victims fight these dangerous narcissists who plan to ruin the lives of their innocent partners. You will successfully come out of stress and disappointments. The effect of many a narcissist has left several love partners ending their lives under messy conditions. Narcissists have significant effects on relationships and not to their benefit. the victims need to change their patterns with these narcissists' abusers. This can only be possible when they escape the narcissist's abuse. You will be able to distinguish yourself from people with this terrible disorder.

According to a variety of studies, narcissism happens mostly in men. The individual has a false sense of self-admiration while seeking excess respect from other people, both known and unknown to them. If not treated in a timely fashion, the condition can translate into more profound side effects. It escalates as far as affecting all people around the person. People affected by the disorder are not capable of tapping into other people's emotional world or showing any form of empathy.

A narcissist quickly flies off the handle at the slightest disagreement. They believe they are the "mighty superhuman" who is to be worshiped and never criticized. Propping up these delusions takes some work; hence, their dysfunctional attitude and behavior tend to stick around. They protect their imagination with defensiveness and rage at the slightest provocation.

Overall, these people are not capable of handling criticism and always disregard how other people feel. To date, this behavior remains a mystery, although a professional can diagnose the condition and treat it with therapy. Having knowledge of the number of people living with a narcissistic disorder offers some comprehension of the situation at hand. Knowledge improves outcomes for people living with this mental condition. The clinical life prevalence of narcissistic personality disorder is at 2-16%, and 1% for the general population. According to studies conducted by Twenge and Campbell 10 years ago, NPD has doubled. Studies also show that 1 in 16 people in the population are living with this condition.

Dealing with a narcissistic personally takes a toll on individuals, both psychologically and emotionally. First encounters with people who display this behavior see them as charmers until you start interacting with them. Be it at work, in a relationship, or as parents with children, you tend to feel some form of suffocation, or struggle with pain and loneliness.

In the end, narcissistic personality disorder has both physiological and physical effects. The physiological effects of NPD can have an immense impact on mental health. Some of them include zero interpersonal skills, hypersensitivity to criticism or insults,

increased feelings of anxiety or depression, and low self-esteem. On the other hand, the physical effects of NPD come from various unhealthy behavior such as an arrogant attitude or behavior, over aggressiveness, the increased risk of abusing alcohol or drugs, and suicidal tendencies.

Since it is not a well-known mental disorder, people live with this condition despite the dire consequences. Seeking treatment is essential for the well-being of the person and their loved ones.

Conclusion

N arcissistic relationships are often complicated; many people who fall prey to narcissists never realize that they were involved in a relationship with a narcissist. There's a lot of information on the internet that explains how narcissism develops, but in order to understand it, it has to be experienced or observed firsthand.

Many of the signs mentioned in this book might not be visible from the outside but can lead to an unhealthy relationship if left unattended. It is also important that we become aware when someone we love is being abused because it can save their lives. Once again, dealing with a narcissist is not an easy task as they are great manipulators. They might start off as a soulmate and then reveal their true colors later on. While many narcissists will promise to love you forever, many will lead you on and leave you when they see an opportunity to get what they want somewhere else. Many people who are in relationships with narcissists tend to be idealistic and very naïve to the dangers of such relationships.

It is important to understand that love can be a very complicated concept, especially in the narcissistic world where everyone is very selfish. We are told from day one as an adult that we are our own person and we don't need anyone else's approval, but we should always strive for our own goals, ideals, ambitions, etc. However, when it comes to love, we might find it hard to understand the concept. Don't let your life become a complete waste by giving in to the narcissist's demands.

CPSIA information can be obtained
at www.ICGtesting.com
Printed in the USA
BVHW091508140621
609529BV00007B/1817